A Doctor's Journe

PHYSICIAN, HEAL THYSELF

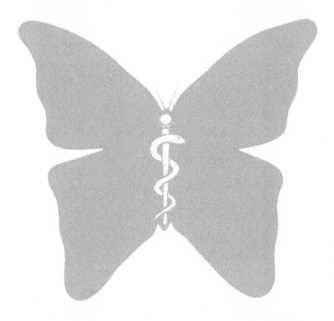

Seema Khaneja, MD

A mindful approach to healing based on teachings of *A Course in Miracles*

ISBN 978-1-7343320-0-1

Library of Congress Control Number 2019920058

All quotes from *A Course in Miracles*, copyright © 2007 by the Foundation for Inner Peace, 448 Ignacio Blvd., #306, Novato, CA 94949, www.acim.org and info@acim.org, are used with permission. Each chapter begins with and may contain quotes from ACIM; the full citation information for these quotes may be found in ACIM Notes at end of the book.

Front cover art by Danielle Mulcahy

Cover layout and design by Sean Mulcahy

Interior layout by Francisca de Zwager

Printed in the United States of America

Published Rochester, New York

Disclaimer and Reader Agreement

Although due diligence has been used in researching and authenticating the information contained in this book, the author makes no representations as to accuracy, completeness, currency, suitability, or validity of any opinions expressed in this book. By reading this book, you, the reader, consent to bear sole responsibility for your own decisions to read or use any of this book's material. The information in this book is shared to support you in your journey to inner peace, and in no way does it constitute medical or mental health advice, nor is this information a substitute for any type of medical or mental health treatment. Should you feel the need for medical help, you are advised to consult with your physician and/or mental health provider. The author shall not be liable for any damages or costs of any type arising out of any action taken by you or others based upon reliance on any materials in this book. However, it is the author's sincere prayer that this book be truly helpful to you.

Visit CoachingForInnerPeace.com

To my dearest Mom, for her undying, steady faith in me, even when mine faltered

To my beloved Papa, for seeing the doctor in me before I even knew what healing was

And to my sweetest Hridesh: may this book be a sturdy bridge that supports you as you embark on your life path.

Acknowledgments

It is said it takes a village to raise a child. Similarly, it takes a village to create a book. I am grateful for all the teachers who showed up on my path to inspire and encourage me:

Morari Bapu - my first spiritual teacher who taught about true love and devotion with a soul-stirring nine-day long recitation of the *Ramayana* (an Indian sacred scripture) held at Jacob Javits Center in New York City (chitrakutdhamtalgajarda.org).

Sri Chinmoy Kumar Ghose - my first teacher of meditation who led me to my first experience of peace and stillness in a small elementary school auditorium in Jamaica, Queens (srichinmoy.org).

My teachers in medicine and teachers I met through my reading, including Deepak Chopra, MD, Bernie Siegel, MD, Louise Hay, Edward Bach, MD, Shakti Gawain, and many others, who helped me to feel that I was not crazy because I knew there was much more to healing than what I was learning in medical school!

The amazing teachers of Vedanta at Arsha Vidya Gurukulam in Pennsylvania and Rishikesh in India (arshavidya.org).

My wonderful teachers of hatha yoga and meditation during my yoga teacher training at the Himalayan Institute in Pennsylvania (himalayaninstitute.org).

The experience of Gyan Vidhi with Pujya Shri Deepak Bhai and all the mahatmas from the Dada Bhagwan Center in New York City and throughout the world (dadabhagwan.org) for teaching me the importance of seeing Pure Soul in myself, others and the universe.

i

Herbert Benson, MD, and all the teachers I met at my very first mind-body clinical training (bensonhenryinstitute.org).

Jim Gordon, MD and all the lovely teachers and fellow students I met at the Center for Mind Body Medicine (cmbm.org).

Peter Gold and Andre Saine, my wonderful teachers and mentors in my practice of homeopathy (and especially Peter who continues to applaud and support my ever-deepening journey into the heart of healing).

Roshi Bodhin Kjolhede and my friends at the Rochester Zen Center (rzc.org) for teaching me by their example about stillness and mindfulness.

Patti Fields, my very first *Course in Miracles* teacher who opened the doors to a whole new way to understand and practice healing (pattifields.com).

David Hoffmeister and all my mighty companions at Living Miracles Monastery and the Mystical Mind Training Program (MMT). I am also grateful to David for his generous permission to use his Levels of Mind diagram (livingmiraclescenter.org).

My mind training partner, Philippe Soule, whom I met through the MMT program for helping me feel free to share and follow my heart's desire to write, create and coach.

My mighty companions in Rochester, New York, for all our wonderful discussions over tea and lunch that nourished me as I worked on this book. Emil Caschetta, Janice McNamara, Molly Wiest Logothetis, Aiko Takemura, Rev. Barbara Adams, and Ray Justice—I love you all!

Lisa Natoli, Bill Free and all the beautiful members I met in the Living in Purpose community. I am so blessed by each of you in helping me feel confident to take steps that led me to where I am today (Teachersofgod.org)

Linda Eaton, at Lifetime Care in Rochester, NY and all the members of the caregiver support group, for providing me with a safe place where I first read chapters from this book. Thank you for reflecting to me the healing power of this book.

Seema Ahmad, my dear high school friend who graciously read through the first draft of the book and was a steady source of encouragement and support.

Judy Morton, my lovely mighty companion who inspires me to live from my heart (authenticallyjudy.com).

My teacher, friend and guide, Veronica Gabrielle La Barrie, for always directing me inward to find all the answers and healing I need (labarrieretreats.org).

My editor and mighty companion, Carol Adler, for understanding and believing in the message of this book right from the start. Thank you for being the loving midwife that allowed this book to be birthed.

Jerry Jampolsky, MD and Trish Ellis for their inspirational teachings and resources of Attitudinal Healing that paved the way for the creation of Coaching for Inner Peace. Jerry's timeless classic, *Love is Letting Go of Fear*, was the gem that first led me to ACIM. (ahinternational.org)

All my clients and readers of my blog at Coaching for Inner Peace for helping me fulfill my mission in healing. Each of you has helped me find greater confidence to share my teachings with a larger audience.

My dear friend, mentor, and publishing wizard, Francisca de Zwager. Our meeting was truly divinely orchestrated. Without your persistence, generosity, and dedication to the art of book publishing, this book would have remained a file confined to my computer. Thank you, dearest Francisca, for setting this book (and me) free! With you, I was able to create the book (both inside and outside) that stayed true to my vision. Bless you for remaining my steadfast companion on this journey.

The Mulcahy family for their love, inspiration, and support. I am grateful to Danielle Mulcahy for sharing her enthusiasm, willingness, and vision in designing the book cover art. Thanks to Kathy, Michael, Sean and Tim Mulcahy, for helping to finalize the cover design. Thanks especially to Michael Mulcahy for taking time to read through the final draft of the manuscript and generously offering his insightful feedback. And a special thanks to my dear friend, Sean Michael Mulcahy, whose music, love, and teachings inspire and nurture me daily. Thank you for painstakingly reviewing with me so many parts of the manuscript and for believing in this book's message of healing. (IAmSeanMichael.com)

Finally, I am so grateful for the inner teacher within my heart. I bow to the inner teacher for allowing this book to come through me, for guiding me lovingly, and for providing me with comfort, refuge and solace always. And to each of you reading this book, I extend my heart's gratitude because I believe you were with me as I wrote this book. Our asking—yours and mine—allowed this book to be birthed.

Namaste,

Seema

Rochester, New York

Preface

Many students first coming to *A Course in Miracles* (ACIM) often express a resistance to the Christian terminology and references to God, Jesus, and Holy Spirit. As Hindus born in India, my first-generation Indian parents raised me on a steady diet of curry, masala chai and God—330 million gods and goddesses, to be precise, which is the official number of gods in the Hindu pantheon. My parents also instilled a value for religious tolerance.

I recall my early childhood days in America when Jehovah's Witnesses regularly showed up at our New York City apartment building, knocking door-to-door. They would share different books and pamphlets about Jesus and the Bible, which became my first introduction to Christianity. I especially enjoyed reading Jesus' parables of healing.

One summer when I was about nine years old, my mom enrolled me in a vacation bible school at a local Presbyterian church where she also volunteered. In her view, whether it is Jesus or the Buddha or Mohammed or Moses or Guru Nanak (from the Sikh faith)—they are all teachers of God, and worthy of our reverence. God is One, she taught me, but His/Her *roop*, the Hindi word for appearance, may be different.

At a young age, my mom taught me that the words used— God, Spirit, Jesus, Allah, Krishna, Durga, or love, peace or the divine—do not matter. Like a finger pointing to the moon, once the moon is seen, there is no need for the finger. Hence, the word is just a symbol for that experience of the deeper truth, which can never be wholly captured by words. *A Course in Miracles* specifically states that "a universal theology is impossible, but a universal experience is not only possible but necessary." The Course is just one path among many that can gently awaken us to who we truly are—infinite love, peace and joy—waiting to be discovered just beneath our limited persona selves.

I am reminded of Lord Krishna from ancient India. When he played the flute, the villagers where he lived simply could not resist the music. They would forget whatever work they were doing so they could just sit and listen. Krishna's flute music was so beautiful and soul-stirring that it transported them out of their normal *doing* reality to an expansive state of *being*.

Although this book, like all others, uses words as a medium of expression, my deepest desire is that you may be lifted beyond the words to a universal experience of love, peace and joy that all the world's spiritual traditions have shared from time immemorial. It is from this space that all miracles flow forth.

Contents

Foreword

I am so very honored to write the foreword for my friend Seema's new book: *Physician, Heal Thyself: A Doctor's Journey from Medicine to Miracles.*

Traditional medicine springs from the traditional scientific method and from empirical study and research, which of course is based on linear time and space and the bodies that inhabit this environment. Alternative methods of healing have evolved in cultures which allow for faith-based approaches and the study and research of consciousness and the mind. There comes a point in spiritual growth and illumination when it dawns that all illness is mental illness, and therefore there are no problems apart from the mind. Another way of stating this insight is that all problems are perceptual problems. Once this is recognized, healing symptoms or healing the body is understood to be a reflection of a change of mind—a decision to change or release all hurtful thoughts.

It is a rare and beautiful experience to behold the causative and creative power of the mind, and through this simple and yet uncompromising recognition to offer the gift of "let healing be". In both medicine and miracles, symptoms are a loud call for healing and for help. The deeper call for healing the mind and healing perception is really a call for a lasting or complete or comprehensive healing, which is to say a stable experience of health and happiness. It requires going down the rabbit hole of spirituality, philosophy, metaphysics, and quantum physics, but the rewards of the discovery are worth it!

For some, including Seema and me, the teachings of *A Course in Miracles* offered a window into the Truth: the Nature or

Essence of our Oneness and Love. Sickness, an expression of fear, can ultimately be seen as nothing more than a call for love and healing. Seema's book offers the reader an opportunity to take the inward journey of discovery toward an actual experience of healed and whole perception. It is possible to have a glimpse of Eternity shining through our awareness, demonstrating and lighting the way to the feeling of Home and Source we have all longed for since time began.

What a wondrous journey to travel from medicine to miracles, lighting the way for helpers of all kinds walking hand in hand and side by side. I rejoice with you along the way of heartfelt gratitude and Joy!

Blessings in all your gentle discoveries,

David Hoffmeister, Director

Foundation for the Awakening Mind
awakening-mind.org

Introduction

Listen, and see if you remember an ancient song you knew so long ago and held more dear than any melody you taught yourself to cherish since.

During the summer following my high school junior year, almost a year before I would enter an accelerated medical school program, I experienced a profound mystical experience while visiting my native India. It was what Abraham Maslow would have referred to as a peak experience, when time stands still and all barriers between *me* and *other* simply dissolve. In that moment, I experienced a sense of completeness and wholeness in which nothing was lacking and there was no need for me to *do* anything.

When I returned to the States, I found myself immersed in the maze of medical school applications, SATs and college essays. Wherever I turned, the voices I heard all seemed to demand that to survive in this world, I needed to make something of myself. Being just as I was—well, that simply was not enough!

Eventually I yielded to this worldly pressure and enrolled in medical school. Yet something about this path never seemed right. I had so many questions that were not being answered in my medical school training. What is healing? What are the roles of thoughts and emotions in healing? What is the role of spirit in healing? How can we support healing? What are the obstacles to healing? What is the role of a doctor in healing? What is *my* purpose in becoming a doctor?

Somehow I knew intuitively that healing lay beyond the body, but all I seemed to be learning was just about the body—organs, tissues, cellular processes, and biochemical pathways. Little by little, all the love, wonder and joy I felt for healing faded away. Instead, as I listened daily in medical school to lectures about deterioration, disease, dying and eventual death, a distinct low-level terror took root in my mind.

I felt like I was living two lives. As a medical student and later resident, I was being trained to constantly look outside to figure out which patient factors needed to be manipulated, such as diet, medications, surgery, and exercise, to achieve optimal health. Yet deep within, whenever I was outside of the confines of medicine, I felt a desire to simply let go of all need to control anything and just give myself over to a life devoted to meditation, prayer and spiritual exploration.

To resolve this conflict, I began to study many different complementary and alternative health modalities. I discovered that most of these healing systems spoke more to the inner psychosocial and spiritual aspects of healing. Often when I should have been studying for exams during medical school, I began to hang out at the self-help and alternative healing sections of my local bookstores and library. Voraciously I read books by Deepak Chopra, MD, Bernie Siegel, MD, Louise Hay, Edward Bach, MD, Shakti Gawain, and others. I attended their workshops and seminars and tried to share this with my medical school friends—most of whom thought I was crazy! I even traveled to India and Nepal, so I could explore yoga and meditation as well as Ayurveda.[1]

All these experiences helped me to nurture my vision of a more expansive healing system that viewed each of us as much more than a soup of biochemical reactions and neurological pathways. Eventually, after completing residency, I settled into my own integrative medical practice where I worked with children and adults facing complex medical and mental health issues. I shared homeopathy, yoga, meditation, Ayurveda and Reiki with them. I found that in cases where the traditional medical model failed to help, many responded favorably to these alternative modalities.

Then one day, I found myself unexpectedly spiraling into a state of deep sadness following a falling out with a dear friend. At the same time, I was facing a personal illness that eventually resulted in chronic pain. Despite all my training in traditional and alternative medicine therapies, nothing seemed to heal my pain. I felt helpless and powerless. It was during this time that I found myself reaching for a book titled *A Course in Miracles*.

This book and its teachings came into my life in my early twenties, during my third year of medical school. It was among the many that I discovered during my regular forays into the healing and spirituality sections of my neighborhood bookstores. At that time, the *Course in Miracles* (ACIM) comforted me but felt remote to my life. The words in the book seemed almost as if they were hieroglyphics. I couldn't relate to them. At the same time, I also had a deep knowing that if I were to go deeper with ACIM, my whole life would change; that prospect frightened me.

Now in my forties, the Course spoke to me like my most trusted friend and advisor. Like soft moonlight that soothes as it shines, the Course drew me out of my depression and taught me about the healing power of forgiveness. As I devoted myself to practicing the teachings of the Course and joining with other Course students and teachers, the light I had been constantly shining on my physical discomfort and emotional turmoil turned inward to the source of my pain, which lay in my perceptions, inside my mind.

I became more interested in discovering what was blocking my peace and joy from within, instead of constantly searching outside for relief in the form of some temporary Band-Aid. Instead of changing what I saw, I committed to change how I was seeing. Gradually, my physical pain disappeared, and this truly was a miracle. Yet I realized that this physical shift was simply a reflection of the deep healing inside my mind, and this was the true miracle.

My inner teacher took me to the heart of healing, and I discovered all the answers I had been seeking since medical school. Eventually this led me to see my whole purpose of being a doctor through a completely different lens.

During my medical training, I understood a physician as someone qualified to practice medicine. But with a deepening practice of ACIM, I realized that a physician can also be defined as a healer. In that sense, we are all physicians because each of us has the capacity and desire to be of service and to help others—which lies at the heart of healing and medicine.

Yet often we are habituated to look outward as if we are healing another person separate from ourselves, or that somehow, someone else has our healing in the form of some external remedy. This is especially the case if we are trained as a physician or other health care professional. We constantly feel that we need to fix another, that they are the broken ones and that we have the expertise to heal them and make them whole again.

But now I could hear an inner voice calling me to awaken to a pathway of healing that was completely the opposite of my medical school training. At the same time, I was not being asked to give up medicine or medications or stop seeing my doctor. Rather, I was being given a more complete vision of healing. From this space, I could clearly see that regardless of the tools used to heal—complementary or traditional, surgery or medications—the key to unlock healing lies in going within. The still small voice gently whispered to me what I needed to hear ever since entering the world of medicine:

Physician, heal thyself by first knowing thyself.

To know myself beyond the limits of my body. To understand myself beyond the persona of the doctor and a limited emotional/mental/intellectual/physical self. To know my family, friends and clients beyond their bodies and their superficial personality selves.

If I could summarize the essence of what I heard inwardly, it would be this:

Physician, heal thyself.

Heal first your perceptions and how you are looking at yourself and this situation. Go within and accept correction of your perception from your inner guide so you can look upon what appears as disease, disorder, devastation or death from the gentle eyes of love. Only then can you truly extend and share healing with others. Otherwise, you are empty and have nothing to offer. Do not remain an unhealed healer, and instead, go within. The plan for healing for each one that comes to you will be given, step by step, but first you need to lay aside all you know. Physician, go within and heal thyself.

Throughout this book, I share what an inward journey of healing can look like while we negotiate an outer challenge. If you are facing a mental and/or physical health issue, I am not suggesting that you discontinue any treatment or stop working with your health care practitioner. Rather, as you read this book, you will come to see that all therapies can be used by our inner teacher for healing. There is a plan for healing with specific steps for each one of us. Yet to hear these steps, we need to get out of our own way and learn to deeply listen to the inner guide within our hearts. I sincerely desire that this book may serve as a bridge to strengthen your connection to your inner guide, for it is this joining that creates healing.

While writing this book, I was also facilitating ACIM groups. Often, I would observe many students struggle with reading *A Course in Miracles*, and many simply would give up, often stating that the language was just too confusing and abstruse. I grew up in the Indian culture; ever since my childhood days I was exposed to storytelling, meditation and music as a common way through which the greatest teachers from the East taught me universal truths. Thus, during our ACIM group meetings, instead of just reading passages from the book, I would introduce the students to relevant movie clips, guided meditations, and contemporary music as well as other devotional Indian music—all with the intention to bring the teachings of ACIM alive. I wanted the students to access these profound and beautiful teachings in a way that was inspirational yet also practical. Being a doctor and trained in complementary healing arts, I would also draw from my medical background to point out that many of the core teachings of ACIM are supported by contemporary scientific research in diverse areas, such as the placebo effect, stress response, quantum physics, and neuroplasticity.

The students in my groups enjoyed being exposed to this multidisciplinary approach. I have written this book in the same way, with a sincere desire to show or illustrate the teachings of ACIM in the context of medicine and healing, rather than simply telling. Therefore, throughout this book, interwoven with references to ACIM teachings, you will find many compelling anecdotes of healing drawn from my personal life as well as from the medical literature. I also share inspiring stories from Indian mythology, music, and movies. Along with the many narratives, I share pertinent scientific research which further supports the validity of ACIM as a powerful manual for healing. I also draw from my background in Eastern spiritual traditions, including Hinduism and Buddhism.

In each chapter, I invite you to be open and willing to shift your perspective about whatever you are facing that is taking you away from your peace, joy and love. This is the miracle — a shift in the way we see ourselves or others, so we can come from a space of more acceptance and less resistance, more openness and less judgment, and more love, and less fear.

In the first two parts of the book, I share my journey of awakening from the outer world of medicine to the inner world of miracles, and all the stepping stones my inner teacher provided for me along the way. These include:

- Research from science including the placebo effect, stress/relaxation response, quantum physics, and neuroplasticity.

- Tools and practices, including mindfulness, prayer, meditation, chanting, listening to the still small voice within our hearts, choosing love over fear, forgiveness, gratitude, being clear about our purpose, connecting with our desire for healing and peace, and joining with our mighty companions.

In the third part of the book, I share my personal experience of chronic illness and how it led me to understand miracles in a way that is practical and relevant to our lives—especially if it involves a chronic challenge.

The final part of the book shares how I ultimately arrived at Coaching for Inner Peace—a way to offer healing that I was searching for ever since entering medical school! Coaching for Inner Peace is a simple, elegant, and practical way to heal our minds[2] so we can experience consistent joy and peace, which I firmly believe is our birthright. This final part can serve as a clear and helpful template, a sort of roadmap for inner peace. Most of us would agree that a peaceful mind is a healthy one, which makes for a healthy physical body, relationships, work life, and life in general!

As you move through this book, you will find that each chapter builds on the previous one. Yet much like a hologram, each chapter also contains the whole message of the book, which is simply an invitation to awaken to your inner guide— to the place of perfect peace, joy, and love deep within each of us. Each chapter can thus serve as a catalyst to allow you to go within and access the healing your mind needs, using the different tools and perspectives provided. This inner healing—the shift from fear to love, from despair to trust, and from separation to connection—is the miracle.

My name Seema means boundary in Hindi. I feel that I was blessed with a life of many boundaries where East and West meet—in my cultural upbringing, in my spiritual exploration, and in my practice of medicine—to perhaps help me discover that truth is one, and to share this truth with others.

I always dreamed about writing a book someday, but never could pin down exactly what it would be about. I believe we are all part of a divine plan and it feels like this book also is part of that plan.

May you feel the immense possibility of healing that is always available to you — and may this book help you experience as many miracles as you need. May it also inspire you to share and extend these miracles to all the lives you touch.

With love, peace and blessings,

Namaste,

Seema

PART ONE

The Search for Healing

CHAPTER 1

Gods, Goddesses, and the World I See

I have invented the world I see.

The gods and goddesses must have listened very attentively on the day I was born in a hospital in a small town in northern India. Papa stood near Mom while the nurse gave me a routine injection. Afterward, as he took me in his arms to comfort me, he made a prophetic announcement.

"Someday my daughter will become a doctor and give injections." Papa spoke with certainty and joy as he proclaimed my destiny.

That was it.

I was only a few hours old and my fate was sealed.

I don't recall when what Papa wanted became what I wanted—or at least what I thought I wanted. But all the essays I wrote since elementary school about what you want to be when you grow up always reflected his wishes. I guess if you write something again and again, you begin to believe it.

When the summer before my senior year in high school arrived, I still intended to become a doctor and by the shortest route possible—a six- or seven-year accelerated medical program. I experienced the typical first-generation immigrant angst to achieve success, which afforded no luxury to find myself at a liberal arts college. All I heard was a ticking clock counting the years until I became the first doctor in my family. In my mind, my life trajectory was clear. After medical school, my parents would arrange my marriage to my soul mate — who of course would be a Bollywood hero facsimile. Children would follow next, and we would settle into uninterrupted domestic and professional bliss thereafter. This was my version of the American dream with obvious Indian overtones.

That summer I planned to volunteer at an animal research laboratory to improve my medical school application. I had little interest in animal research or laboratories, yet I felt an inner compulsion to do whatever was needed to enhance my medical school application.

Then my parents dropped a bombshell.

We were going to India that summer to visit relatives and perform a pilgrimage. There was no room for discussion. Before I knew it, we landed in New Delhi, where the summer temperature averages 110 degrees Fahrenheit. Air conditioning in those days was non-existent or, at best, a machine called a cooler that sprayed cool water into a room. And that was assuming the electricity didn't go out.

Nothing in India ran on time — from the trains to the buses to the never-ending parade of visitors. It was common to joke about EST, PST, and IST, or Indian Standard Time. But amazingly the one thing that departed with punctual regularity every evening was the electricity, with lapses of several hours at a time. This, I soon learned, was the norm. I was miserable, and I made sure everyone knew I was miserable. No matter how many times I showered, the heat was simply oppressive. I felt like I was being baked in an oven. I also felt emotionally isolated. I felt nothing in common with my cousins or other relatives.

When the time for the pilgrimage came, my mom was unable to go since she wanted to spend time with her ailing mother. Papa was already back in the U.S. to begin a new job. So, my cousins and I, along with our uncle, began a journey to Vaishno Devi, a shrine located inside a cave in the hills of Jammu and Kashmir at a height of about 5200 feet. The journey involved a train and bus ride, with the last 12 kilometers by foot. In those days there were no guard rails. While the others we met along the path would chant Jai Mata Di (Victory to the Goddess), my thoughts were more along the lines of, *We are going to die. We're all going to fall over the edge and simply die!* There was no trace of any spiritual or devotional feeling in my mind.

When we finally reached the shrine, we were surrounded by hundreds of others also waiting for *darshan*[3] inside the cave. Everyone was pushing and shoving so they could enter first. As the sun reached its zenith, my mind also heated up with flares of judgment at the hypocrisy of the situation — humans fighting to worship rocks while not showing any respect for each another.

Then something happened once we stepped inside the cave. Perhaps it was the reprieve from the oppressive heat.

Perhaps it was the cool water that flowed under my feet.

Perhaps it was not dealing with the crowds anymore.

We saw the three Pindies, or stones atop a five-and-a-half-foot tall rock that legend states are a manifestation of the Goddess Vaishnaivi when she shed her human form. But honestly, I don't recall them. I simply know that for the first time ever, my mind's incessant chatter ceased. I was flooded by a peace so deep that all my irritation and impatience were washed away. I touched the water with my hands and instinctively brought it to touch my forehead and lips in reverence. Somehow it felt holy. I felt holy. I felt whole. I was complete.

When I returned to the States, I was not the same. My friends commented that I smiled more. I seemed happier, less introverted and more outgoing. While I continued the medical school application maze, I also heard a soft, gentle voice stir within my heart, calling me to another way. I enrolled in a metaphysics class and pondered deeply over Herman Hesse's *Siddhartha*. I completed my senior thesis project on the *Bhagavad Gita*. I felt inspired to meditate, chant, pray and read about saints and mystics past and present—Mother Teresa, Gandhi, St. Francis, Krishna, Sri Aurobindo, Kabir, and others. I joined my high school friends and organized a charity bake sale for starving children in Ethiopia. Eagerly I read Indian news magazines and empathized with India through the Union Carbide gas leak fiasco and the assassination of then Indian Prime Minister Indira Gandhi.

Suddenly, medical school seemed very remote and limiting, like a speck on a map while a whole other galaxy waited to be explored, tasted, and experienced.

At the same time, another voice cautioned me: *You silly girl! This foolishness will lead you nowhere. Forget it! What you really need to do is focus and study harder, so you make something of yourself.*

During this time of confusion dawned another day when the gods and goddesses must have listened attentively once more. Papa and I were riding the subway train together. He was headed to work, and I was on my way to my high school in Manhattan.

"Papa, I've been thinking. Maybe I could do something different instead of medicine." I spoke to Papa hesitantly, somewhat timidly.

Papa continued reading his newspaper, but I knew he was listening.

"I mean something like writing or journalism. And then apply to medical school later." The words tumbled out very fast now. I braced myself for his reply.

Papa folded his paper, in anticipation of his stop. He turned and looked at me. He spoke quietly yet firmly. "Journalism and writing—these are not suitable professions for women. Medicine is a noble and honorable profession. It will be good for you."

We arrived at Papa's stop. He got up. "Good luck on your chemistry exam."

The doors of the train opened and soon Papa was gone, his figure indistinguishable from the hundreds of other exiting passengers.

I sighed. I knew we would not discuss this matter again. Papa was a man of few words that were usually set in stone. I also knew my mother would defer to Papa, in keeping with Indian tradition. Yet as I reflected on Papa's words, I felt a force operating stronger than me or my parents. For a moment, I became the observer. At the ripe age of 17, I saw a stream flowing, and I was flowing right along with it, straight to medical school, with no stops in between.

During the first year of medical college, I dreamed of a white ceramic toilet bowl overflowing with blood. The blood slowly seeped outward while I stood by, helpless and paralyzed. That same year I developed iron-deficiency anemia and vertigo. My family physician attributed this to my recent transition to a vegetarian diet. Although I modified my diet and started some iron supplements, intuitively I knew this anemia reflected my deep inner conflict.

From an academic perspective, I did not find medical school difficult. I was a good student and enjoyed studying, so I didn't flunk out. Yet medicine simply didn't inspire me. Where was medicine's soul? Its spirit? Surely it could not be found in dissecting dead cadavers and memorizing hundreds of biochemical pathways. Moreover, I was haunted by a nagging doubt that I was forgetting my true purpose and was becoming a doctor only because of parental obligation. Yet even when I saw my best friend leave our medical school program to pursue a career in literature, I didn't feel free to abandon my path.

Every year the decision to stay or leave weighed heavily on me. I felt burdened by my parents' sacrifice to raise and educate me in America, thousands of miles away from all they had left behind in India. I wanted to be the obedient "good little Indian girl." Also, at some level I trusted my parents knew my best interests. Eventually I surrendered to the path of medicine as my destiny. The soft, gentle voice paled in contrast to the loud demands to succeed in medical exams, please my parents, and make something of myself.

At school and on the hospital wards, I fulfilled my duties with a smiling face and earned rave reviews from my professors and colleagues. At home, I alternated between sullen

8

withdrawal and frequent angry explosions. My experience was painful and fraught with struggle.

Yet as I write this today, I clearly understand this was a perfect reflection of my mind at that time.

I have invented the world I see.

Once I discovered *A Course in Miracles* (ACIM) and as I went deeper with the teachings, I began to realize that the world I saw during that time as a young medical student was like a huge Dolby panoramic screen—reflecting concepts about sacrifice, guilt, and unworthiness, as well as parent-child responsibility and obligation. When we watch a movie inside a theater, we accept that the screen is simply a reflection of the film inside the projector. In the same way, the world I perceived reflected back to me the thoughts and beliefs I held inside my mind. We know it is the film that produces the images projected outward on the movie screen; similarly, it is my thoughts and beliefs that form my perception or experience of my life. Moreover, just as the light is always present in the projector, the light of spirit is always present within my mind. The film, however—which is often some false understanding about me or another—needs to be exposed and released to experience this light.

According to the Course, the split mind I experienced—a mind in conflict with itself—is what we all bring to the world. The split mind forgets its inherent love, peace, and joy, and buries its power of choice under teeming layers of fear, doubt, guilt, and unworthiness. Instead of seeing the cause inside my mind, I was perceiving myself to be a victim of external events. I experienced what ACIM refers to as a *grievance*, so I continued to blame my parents and the world of medicine. I even saw God as vindictive and demanding sacrifice.

One of the earliest messages I received in my mind after coming to the Course began to dismantle the idea of God as punishing and wrathful:

> *I am not the God of your past learning. I come not to take away but replenish and restore. Lean your head on me, sweet child. There is nothing more you need to do.*

In my medical school career, within the drama of blame, powerlessness and helplessness, my inner guide continued to send many experiences to awaken me. The placebo effect was one such touchstone that was a beacon of light to rekindle my awareness of the immense power of the mind to choose and align with healing or *dis*-ease.

CHAPTER 2

The Placebo Effect: Discovering the Power of the Mind

I have given everything I see... all the meaning that it has for me.

Early in medical school I became fascinated by the placebo effect—that an inactive substance like a sugar pill that appears identical to the active medication could improve a patient's condition simply because of their belief and expectation to heal! The more I read, the more excited I became. However, often I felt alone. Nearly all my medical buddies were mesmerized with Western biomedicine. They poked fun at me, predicting that I would tell my patients their ailments were in their minds, or all in their heads.

During my medical school career in the late 1980s, most conventionally trained Western physicians viewed the placebo effect as a nuisance. It could mess up results of clinical drug trials designed for determining the effectiveness of a specific medicine in treating high blood pressure, asthma, or some other ailment. With the placebo effect operating, a certain percentage of the patients or research participants taking the drugs would get better anyway, regardless of the effectiveness of the drug.

I always wondered why that was a bad thing. If some patients were going to get better anyway because of the placebo effect, why would we as physicians and scientists not want to explore this further? While I was researching material for this chapter, I was happy to learn that in 2012, Harvard Medical School, along with several Harvard-affiliated hospitals, created the Program in Placebo Studies and the Therapeutic Encounter (PiPS), headquartered at Beth Israel Deaconess Medical Center. This reflects changing attitudes in Western medicine—that there is value in studying not *whether* the placebo works, but rather, *how* it works.[4] As I write this today, the young medical student inside me feels a sense of being finally heard and validated, instead of feeling belittled and dismissed.

Brief History and Origin of the Placebo Effect

The first documented medical use of the word placebo (Latin for "I shall please") dates to the late 18th century. A placebo treatment was given more to please and comfort a patient than to bring about any change in pathophysiology. Physicians often even held negative value judgments about the placebo effect. It was thought to be more effective for patients who were deemed less intelligent, neurotic, or otherwise inadequate.[5]

The scientific study of the placebo effect is usually attributed to Henry Beecher.[6] While working as a physician in World War II, Beecher ran out of pain-killing morphine and replaced it with a simple saline solution but continued telling the wounded soldiers it was morphine.[7] To his surprise, the soldiers still reported reduction or even relief of pain. In 1955, Beecher published his groundbreaking paper, "The Powerful Placebo," in which he concluded from the studies he reviewed that an average of 35% of patients responded to placebo.[8] Modern day research demonstrates that the placebo effect can range anywhere from 10 to 100% across many different conditions, including irritable bowel syndrome, migraine headaches, asthma, nausea, anxiety, and chronic pain.[9]

Tumors that Melt Away

A case history of "Mr. Wright" in 1957 clearly illustrates the power not only of the placebo effect but also of the opposite, or nocebo effect (Latin for "I shall harm").[10] This is a phenomenon whereby inactive substances—or mere suggestions of potential side effects of substances—actually bring about negative effects in a patient.[11] Both placebo and nocebo effects arise from the patient's mind, specifically their positive or negative beliefs and expectations about how a particular substance will affect them.

Mr. Wright suffered from advanced lymphosarcoma and was hospitalized in California.[12] He had exhausted all treatment options and was given only days to live. His neck, armpits, chest, abdomen and groin were filled with tumors the size of oranges. His spleen and liver were enormous. Every other day, one to two liters of milky fluid were drained from his chest. But Mr. Wright didn't want to die. He heard about an exciting new drug called Krebiozen prepared from horse serum. He begged his physician, Dr. Philip West, to try it. At first his doctor refused because the drug was only being tried on people with a life expectancy of at least three months. But Mr. Wright was persistent, so Dr. West finally relented. On a Friday, he gave Wright an injection of Krebiozen, not expecting him to survive the weekend because he was "febrile, gasping for air, (and) completely bedridden."[13]

To Dr. West's surprise, on the following Monday, Mr. Wright was "walking around the ward, chatting happily with the nurses, spreading his good cheer to any who would listen."[14]

When Dr. West examined the other patients who received Krebiozen treatment, he discovered no change or further deterioration. Only Mr. Wright responded! Dr. West wrote that Mr. Wright's tumors "melted like snowballs on a hot stove" and were half their original size.[15] This was a far more rapid decrease in size than *even the strongest X-ray radiation treatments could have accomplished.*

Ten days later, after receiving three injections of Krebiozen weekly, Mr. Wright was discharged from the hospital. As far as his doctors could tell, he was cancer free. Previously "gasping his last breath through an oxygen mask, (he) was now not only breathing normally, and fully active, he took off in his plane, at 12,000 feet, with no discomfort!"[16]

Mr. Wright remained well for about two months. Then articles appeared asserting that Krebiozen had no effect on lymph node cancer. Mr. Wright became disturbed by these reports. According to Dr. West, Wright had innate optimism but was also "reasonably logical and scientific in his thinking."[17] He began to lose faith in his treatment, became very depressed, suffered a relapse, and was readmitted to the hospital. This time Dr. West tried an experiment. He told Mr. Wright not to believe the news reports, because this version of the drug had a limited shelf life before it began to lose its effectiveness. However, he told Mr. Wright that he had a new highly concentrated version of the drug that was to arrive tomorrow and he wanted to treat him again. Mr. Wright agreed and "became his optimistic self again, eager to start over... and his faith was very strong."[18] To create the proper atmosphere, Dr. West went through an elaborate ritual before injecting him with "fresh water and nothing more" while telling him he was actually receiving treatment.[19] The results were again dramatic. Tumors melted, chest fluid vanished, and Mr. Wright was once again the "picture of health."[20] Dr. West continued the water injections and Mr. Wright resumed flying. He remained symptom-free for another two months.

Shortly after, however, Mr. Wright heard reports from the American Medical Association that a nationwide study of Krebiozen found the drug worthless in the treatment of cancer. This time Wright's faith was completely broken. He died two days later.

In my medical training, I learned that a case such as Mr. Wright's is considered anecdotal evidence, just a mere story that may be interesting and even entertaining yet cannot be considered on the same level as scientific data derived from carefully conducted experiments. This idea never sat well with me. It was like someone had just punctured my balloon and I could no longer soar free in the realm of possibility.

To me, Mr. Wright's story and similar cases highlight all we still need to understand about the power of the mind to heal or not heal, based on its chosen version of so-called reality. If we focus on the inefficacy of Krebiozen for treating cancer or dismiss the case as unique, we miss the key point. When Mr. Wright believed Krebiozen was helpful, he experienced healing in his body not once but twice. The opposite effect also occurred twice when Mr. Wright lost faith in his therapy, first with his relapse and the tumor returning, and then with his eventual death. One person's experience of their ability of the mind to either heal or succumb to disease can be instructive for all of us—if we are willing to listen and learn.

Further Placebo Research

Fortunately, many other scientists have also researched the placebo effect. In 1962, Japanese researchers took a group of

15- to 18-year-old males who were extremely allergic to poison ivy and rubbed one forearm of each boy with a poison ivy leaf but told them it was harmless.[21] As a control, they rubbed the boy's other forearm with a harmless leaf that they claimed was poison ivy. All the boys developed a rash on the arm rubbed with the harmless leaf that they believed was poison ivy and 11 of the 13 boys developed no rash at all where the poison ivy had touched them.

Today, such a study would not be performed for obvious ethical reasons. However, this study does question the widely accepted notion that if we have an allergic reaction, it is simply because we were exposed to the allergic substance. This study, even if it is small, demonstrates that for most of the boys, it was the *meaning* or *interpretation* they assigned to the leaf—based on whether they *believed* it was harmful or harmless—that determined their reaction.

Psychologist Irving Kirsch, PhD, who currently serves as the Associate Director of the Program in Placebo Studies at Harvard, has been studying the placebo effect for over 30 years. Dr. Kirsch is the originator of the expectancy theory, based on the idea that people's experiences depend partly on their expectations.[22] According to Kirsch, this is the process that lies behind the placebo effect. Dr. Kirsch and his colleagues have also shown that the placebo effect can operate in the treatment of mental health conditions, such as depression—meaning that most of the improvement in patients taking an antidepressant is due to the placebo effect.[23,24]

Amazingly, the placebo effect can even operate in the realm of surgery. This is referred to as sham or placebo surgery. Let's say that a surgeon tells their patient they will receive an operation that will reduce their chest pain from angina[25,26] or diminish knee pain from osteoarthritis[27] or from a torn meniscus.[28] When patients believe they have undergone an operation that their surgeons told them would be helpful, they will feel better *even if they never had the actual procedure —* meaning they had just received a skin incision to the chest or the knee but nothing more. How amazing is that?

A 2010 Harvard study further confirms that placebo can work *even when* people know they are taking it. Forty patients with irritable bowel syndrome (IBS) were given a bottle clearly labeled *placebo pills*. They were informed that this bottle contained pills made of inactive substances, such as sugar pills that "have been shown in clinical studies to produce significant improvement in IBS symptoms through mind-body self-healing processes."[29] A second group of 40 IBS patients were given no pills and served as the control group. After three weeks, the group taking the placebo pills reported twice as much relief as the control group.

The Healing Power of Our Minds

To me, these studies question the belief that therapies themselves are inherently helpful or harmful. Regardless of receiving sham surgery or the real thing, taking a placebo pill or active medication, or even being subjected to a supposedly harmful stimulus such as poison ivy, *it is the meaning and interpretation that each patient chooses and the expectation they have that seem to be the key factors in determining their experience.*

I have given everything I see… all the meaning that it has for me.

It is this place of choice and decision-making in the mind— both at conscious and subconscious levels—that I want to explore further with you as we move through this book.

If you are taking medications or using supplements to support your healing, I am not suggesting that you stop them. Each of us is walking a path of healing that often includes external agents, such as prescription drugs and surgery. Rather, my desire is that you leave this chapter willing to *see yourself as a powerful agent of healing* because of your power to choose how you see yourself and your world. This world includes medicine, healing, supplements, and so forth. Based on all my personal and professional experience as well as my research, I firmly believe that our perception of ourselves and of the therapies we use is fundamental to *all* healing.

In the next chapter, we further discuss the power of our minds by looking more deeply at mind-body medicine and the stress response.

CHAPTER 3

To Love or Fear, That Is the Real Question

*You have but two emotions (love or fear), and one you made
and one was given you. Each is a way of seeing, and different
worlds arise from their different sights.*

Although intuitively I knew the true essence of healing
resides in the mind, I felt impelled to study mind-body
medicine further to reinforce this inner knowing. When I refer
to the mind, I include the total experience of our thoughts,
beliefs, emotions, and perceptions, as well as our conscious
and subconscious desires. Mind-body medicine explores the
scientific basis of the interconnectedness of our thoughts,
sensations, and feelings, and of our mind, body, and spirit.[30]

What Is the Stress Response? How Does It Work?

One of the basic scientific underpinnings of mind-body
medicine is the stress (fight-or-flight) response. This is an
evolutionary mechanism that we share with other mammals
and activate whenever we encounter any situation we
perceive as stressful. This response helps mobilize our bodies
and energy stores to fight an oncoming threat or run away
and take flight.[31]

In earlier times when we were still hunters and gatherers, this
response was invaluable—especially if we were hunting prey
that could turn the tables on us, making us the hunted prey!
Unfortunately, these days we engage the stress response to

cope with stressors that are not life-threatening, such as traffic jams, work pressure, and relationship difficulties.

Allow me to illustrate with an example from my own life. Let's say I'm driving in snowy weather during the winter months in Rochester, NY, where I live. As a baseline, I don't particularly enjoy winter driving, especially during the night. So, from the beginning, I perceive this situation as stressful. Now, imagine that my car starts to skid, and I think that I may hit another vehicle. Immediately, my mind triggers a fear response. The amygdala, which is the part of my brain that contributes to emotional processing, sends a distress signal to the hypothalamus.[32] This is the area of the brain that is considered the command center, about the size of an almond that lies at the base of the brain.[33] The hypothalamus connects the endocrine system with the autonomic nervous system, which controls such involuntary body functions as breathing, blood pressure, and the heartbeat.

The autonomic nervous system has two components, the sympathetic and the parasympathetic nervous system.[34] The sympathetic nervous system is like the gas pedal in a car. It triggers the fight-or-flight response, providing the body with a burst of energy that allows it to respond to perceived dangers—by either fighting through them or fleeing and escaping to safety. The parasympathetic nervous system acts like a brake. It promotes the rest and digest response that calms the body after the danger has passed.

In my hypothetical situation, after my amygdala sends a distress signal, my hypothalamus activates my sympathetic nervous system by sending signals through the autonomic nerves to my adrenal glands located on top of my kidneys. These glands respond by pumping the hormone epinephrine (also known as adrenaline) into my bloodstream.

As epinephrine circulates throughout my body, several changes occur. My heart beats faster than normal, pushing blood to the peripheral muscles of my legs and arms, as well as my heart, brain and other vital organs. My pulse rate and blood pressure go up. I also start to breathe more rapidly as the small airways in my lungs open wide, so I can take in as much oxygen as possible with each breath. Extra oxygen is sent to my brain so I am alert, and my sight, hearing, and other senses also become sharper. Meanwhile, epinephrine triggers the release of blood sugar and fats from temporary storage sites in the body. These nutrients flood my bloodstream, supplying energy to all parts of my body.

These changes happen so quickly, I am not even aware of them. In fact, research shows that the wiring is so efficient, the amygdala and hypothalamus start this cascade *even before* the brain's visual centers can fully process what is happening. That's why people can jump out of the path of an oncoming car even before they think about what they are doing.

Here is a diagram that illustrates what is happening:

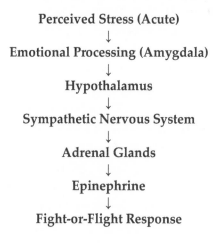

Perceived Stress (Acute)
↓
Emotional Processing (Amygdala)
↓
Hypothalamus
↓
Sympathetic Nervous System
↓
Adrenal Glands
↓
Epinephrine
↓
Fight-or-Flight Response

Now, let's say the car skids but I have taken my foot off the gas pedal, so eventually it stops by the side of the road. I don't collide with another car and I am safe. Even the car is fine with little or no damage. The stress has passed so my fear dissipates. Now my parasympathetic nervous system takes over and acts like a brake. My breathing slows down, along with my blood pressure and pulse. The danger has passed; I can relax and let go.

Chronic Stress: Always Being on Guard

This is what happens when a perceived threat passes quickly. But what about chronic stress? What happens in situations involving divorce, chronic illness, losing a job, experiencing major financial losses, or caring for a loved one who is chronically or terminally ill? What about grieving the death of a loved one, or even just feeling constantly overwhelmed by the responsibilities of day-to-day life, juggling family and work?

In these cases, the hypothalamus activates a second component of the stress response system, known as the HPA axis. This network consists of the hypothalamus, the pituitary gland, and the adrenal glands. The pituitary gland is a pea-sized structure located at the base of the brain, just below the hypothalamus and attached to it by nerve fibers. If we continue to perceive a dangerous or stressful situation, then the hypothalamus will start to release the corticotropin-releasing hormone (CRH). The CRH travels to the pituitary gland, triggering the release of the adrenocorticotropic hormone (ACTH). This hormone travels to the adrenal glands, prompting them to release cortisol. The body thus stays revved up and on high alert. If we were to illustrate this cascade of hormone release, here is what it would look like:

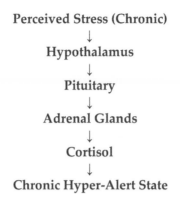

Perceived Stress (Chronic)
↓
Hypothalamus
↓
Pituitary
↓
Adrenal Glands
↓
Cortisol
↓
Chronic Hyper-Alert State

What Happens if We Simply Freeze?

Recently, many researchers have modified the stress response to include the fight-flight-or-freeze response.[35] For example, perhaps we are facing some stressful situation that leaves us feeling so overwhelmed that we may become numb and rigid, like a deer that freezes in front of the bright headlights of an oncoming car.

The freeze response can happen in situations of rape, car accidents, being robbed at gunpoint, or during other such traumatic events. The person experiencing such a situation can feel terrified and see no hope of survival. They may pass out, become rigid, or mentally exit the situation, thus feeling removed from their body and any sensation of pain. Later they may not recall any details of the event or that it even occurred.

Like the fight-or-flight response, the freeze response in the short-term may have some adaptive value. A person experiencing extreme trauma, such as witnessing chronic domestic abuse as a child, may be able to numb themselves to survive the situation because they couldn't fight or flee.

However, if the freeze response is not brought to conscious awareness for healing, then later in life as an adult, it can lead to long-term emotional distress in the form of PTSD (post-traumatic stress disorder). The suppressed fear or panic linked to the memory of the childhood trauma can cause an extreme reaction to a current trigger that is disproportionate—as if what occurred in the past is happening all over again.

For example, imagine a child growing up in a family system in which everyone is always yelling and arguing. The child finds a way to shut this out by disappearing mentally and emotionally and distancing themselves from the situation. As an adult, they may experience fear of intimate friendships or relationships. If they face even a minor disagreement, they may feel an extreme sense of fear or panic. This would happen because the current situation triggers buried painful emotions associated with a previous experience that has not been fully processed and healed.

The Effects of Chronic Stress on the Mind and Body

The stress response is believed to have developed as a survival mechanism to help our prehistoric ancestors react quickly to life-threatening situations while hunting for their food. If we need to fight off a threat, or flee to safety, or freeze to protect ourselves from some trauma, we can understand the need for a precisely orchestrated and nearly instantaneous sequence of hormonal changes and physiological responses. However, what happens when we experience stress all the time?

When I entered medical school, I learned that stress was a major factor in possibly 50% of all medical illnesses. Today almost 75 to 90 percent of all visits to primary health care providers are due to stress-related problems.[36] Chronic stress takes a toll on the mind and body that contributes to many health problems. Are you ready for the list?[37]

- High blood pressure, elevated heart rate, and coronary heart disease
- Obesity
- Respiratory disorders, including asthma
- Cirrhosis of the liver
- Diabetes
- Chronic musculoskeletal pain, including neck and back pain
- Allergic reactions and eczema
- Headaches, including migraine headaches
- Autoimmune diseases, including rheumatoid arthritis
- Overeating comfort foods or not eating enough
- Irritable bowel syndrome, gastrointestinal ulcers, and ulcerative colitis
- Illness due to suppression of the immune system
- Cancer
- Erectile dysfunction
- Fertility problems
- Low sex drive
- Irregular menstrual periods
- Fatigue
- Accidental injury
- Schizophrenia
- Anxiety
- Depression
- Alcohol or drug abuse/addiction
- Social withdrawal
- Insomnia
- Suicide

Research shows that even diseases that were thought to have a purely genetic basis can manifest differently in identical twins who share the same genetic material.[38] Scientists believe this is partly due to epigenetics—the process whereby external mechanisms, such as lifestyle factors, including diet, exercise and stress, can switch genes on and off through different chemical modifications.

Can We Ever Be Free of Stress in Our Modern Day Lives?

Usually when I share this information about the stress response in group seminars, I feel a cloak of heaviness settle over the audience. Stress seems to be a ubiquitous part of our lives. How can we ever escape it without renouncing the modern world of iPhones, Facebook, and the Internet, or perhaps moving permanently to a monastery in the Himalayan Mountains?

Fortunately, we do have another choice. The parasympathetic nervous system, the brake pedal, allows us to rest, relax and let go. Returning to my initial scenario, when I remove my foot from the gas pedal and the car eventually comes to a stop, the emergency has passed. The fire is out. My heart rate and blood pressure return to normal and my breathing is no longer shallow and frenetic. My neck and shoulder muscles can slowly relax because the burden of worry and fear begins to diminish.

Dr. Herbert Benson, a cardiologist who is currently the Director Emeritus of the Benson-Henry Institute for Mind Body Medicine at Massachusetts General Hospital, first coined the term "relaxation response" (RR) in the 1970s when he and his team of researchers studied the effect of meditation on volunteers while clinically measuring their metabolism, their rate of breathing, and their brain waves.[39] The relaxation response engages the parasympathetic nervous system and is the opposite of the stress response which is orchestrated by the sympathetic nervous system. Benson and his team discovered dramatic physiological changes during states of meditation. Essentially, the body slowed down with decreased metabolism and a slowing of both breathing and heart rates. In addition, the subjects' brain waves changed to the relaxing theta wave pattern.

We can elicit the relaxation response in a number of ways, including deep abdominal breathing, focus on or chanting a soothing word (such as love or peace), visualization of tranquil scenes, progressive muscle relaxation, energy healing, acupuncture, massage, prayer, meditation, tai chi, qi gong, and yoga.[40] If the relaxation response is practiced on a regular basis, the body performs its routine maintenance easily, including digestion, internal repair, and regeneration and healing.

Benson's laboratory, along with many other researchers in mind-body medicine, have shown that the relaxation response is effective therapy for many different stress-related disorders, including anxiety, mild and moderate depression, chronic anger and hostility, insomnia, high blood pressure, premenstrual tension, menstrual cramps, rheumatoid arthritis, and irritable bowel syndrome.[41]

My Power of Choice Lies in My Perception

For us to experience ourselves as powerful agents of healing, we need to recognize that the first step in the cascade of the stress response is *our perception of the situation*. Previously I shared that I experience driving in the snow as stressful, whereas someone else may not mind driving in these conditions. The teachings of *A Course in Miracles* take us directly to the root of the stress response—which lies in the perception, or interpretation of our situation. Once the stress response has started, it is like the horse that has escaped from the barn. We can chase after it, but it will require much more energy to bring it back to the barn. However, if we can become aware of our perceptions, we then have a choice to see our situation differently.

So, What Are Our Choices?

I am sitting at my local Barnes and Noble cafe as I write this. I am always amazed by how many beverage choices I have: chai, coffee, tea, water, juice, smoothies, espresso, cappuccino, and so much more. Then there are choices within choices. If I decide on tea, I still need to decide whether I want decaf or caffeinated, if I want milk and what kind of milk, and if I want to add sugar, a sugar substitute, or honey. We would like to think we have as many choices in the mind as well. Certainly, while doing my medical school psychiatry clerkship, I learned from the *Diagnostic and Statistical Manual of Mental Disorders* (*DSM*) many complex classifications of different mental, emotional and psychological states, ranging from psychosis to depression to anxiety.

We may think that there are as many perceptions as there are people inhabiting the planet. This would not be entirely untrue. Yet this is what I love about *A Course in Miracles*; it simplifies our life by helping us understand that every perception we experience about any situation we face arises from only two lenses or choices. Those two choices are either love or fear, originating respectively in the *awake and aware mind* or the *sleeping and unaware ego-mind*.[42]

Who Is My Teacher? Whom Do I Believe?

We are convinced by the ego mind that we are divorced and forever abandoned by our inner knowing, the place within us that is wise, peaceful and joyous, regardless of our external circumstances. If we feel disconnected from our Source or true Self, this naturally gives rise to a chronic, underlying fear and anxiety with an accompanying deep sense of abandonment, loss, shame, guilt and unworthiness. The Buddhists describe this condition as being "a child of rich birth wandering poor on this earth" with a begging bowl. [43]

Like the story of the prodigal son who leaves his father's home and squanders away all his wealth, we are afraid to go home lest we be punished. Yet a part of our mind is still awake and aware; it has not forgotten our connection to love and peace. We always have the choice to view the world and ourselves through this lens. If we do make this choice, we will see a completely different world—not because the world changes but because *we make a decision to change the way we see the world.*

Eventually, the prodigal son decides that even if his father will only grant him the status of a servant in his home, that would be better than the poverty, loss and desolation he is facing. He remembers that he still has a home he can return to—that he has a connection to his father that cannot be changed, regardless of his current circumstances. What he does not expect is that upon his return, his father welcomes him with a feast and much celebration. The son discovers he is and always has been loved, cherished and adored. His father doesn't care how he looks, or what he has done or not done. All that matters is that he is still alive. Finally, he has returned to the family fold. In the parable of the prodigal son, the father is a beautiful symbol of the unconditional love that is *always* available to us.

If we now apply the framework of ACIM to the stress response, we can see that it is essentially a reaction out of fear and alarm, whereas the relaxation response allows for moments of rest and letting go. We literally see the world differently as we remove the ego lens of fear. Now we see with the eyes of love. Fear creates separation while love allows our minds and hearts to join with the experience before us. We allow ourselves to finally breathe. From this space, we discover creative ways to resolve our problems and find a way to move forward that feels better than our previous coping mechanisms.

When we practice the Course workbook lessons consistently, we become adept at the practice of mind watching. We step back and simply witness all the thought forms in our mind as they arise, without any judgment or effort on our part to fix, change or improve them. Slowly we realize that we *can* choose the direction of our thoughts. We can even ask for help from our inner guide to direct our thoughts to those that bring us peace and a sense of comfort and safety.

In my own experience when driving in snow, I have observed that if I can focus on the beauty of the snowflakes as they swirl in front of the windshield, I can relax into the driving. Although I cannot control the car by predicting beforehand whether it will skid, I am able to experience a more grounded, settled, and less fearful experience. As I feel a greater sense of security, I find my reaction to any potential danger also improves. Once again, this feeling of safety arises from a space of relaxation and comfort—not from fear, which would only create more panic.

A *Course in Miracles* further empowers and liberates our minds by teaching us that the emotion of fear is a man-made phenomenon. It is not of God. To allow love and peace to flow in, we don't need to find love or somehow create peace. The Course teaches us that *we are already the love and peace we seek.* We simply need to be willing to recognize this. We need to stop believing the voice of fear and claim our divine inheritance of love, peace and joy. Yet, how did we get into this predicament in the first place? How did we forget our true identity? We will explore this in the next chapter.

CHAPTER 4

Maya, Dreaming, and the Big Bang: Did the Separation Really Occur?

The world is an illusion. Those who choose to come to it are seeking for a place where they can be illusions, and avoid their own reality. Yet when they find their own reality is even here, then they step back and let it lead the way. What other choice is really theirs to make? To let illusions walk ahead of truth is madness. But to let illusion sink behind the truth and let the truth stand forth as what it is, is merely sanity.

When we dream, we fully believe everything we see — the dream figures and what they say and do. The whole story seems very real to us. We dream of heroes and villains as well as victims and victimizers. We only realize it's a dream when we awaken.

Yet what if when we awaken from our nightly sleep, we enter another dream world? What if the world we perceive with our senses — what we hear with our ears and see with our eyes — is not the real world? What if there's something more than this linear world of time and space where we live and breathe each day?

ACIM teaches that even while we are awake, whenever we perceive through the ego lens of fear, we are dreaming a dream of separation. Look at the world around us. If we watch the news, we witness fearful images and terrorizing events. In our personal lives, who among us has not experienced some loss, pain, or even an acute sense of being isolated and alone? The Course wants to gently awaken us from this fearful experience of the world to give us happy dreams of forgiveness—those dreams that open us up to an experience of steady love that does not waver with the season or wane with the setting sun.

That we are dreaming even when we are awake is a profound concept that is both non-dualistic and non-linear; it cannot be understood intellectually. Yet often as beginning Course students, we may use this idea without any personal experience. In this chapter and chapter 5, we will explore the metaphysical foundation of this concept, supporting our findings with references to science, movies, music, passages from Eastern scriptures, and from the Course itself.

Maya, Krishna and Narada

As a young girl, I often heard my parents and elder relatives talk about how we are all in the grips of *maya*, or the illusory nature of life. Yet the concept of *maya* never made sense. My mom shared a beautiful story to help me understand.

Narada, a very famous Indian sage once visited Lord Krishna. "Krishna, what is *maya*?"

"Narada, the answer you seek cannot be given in words. It must be experienced. Come, take a walk with me."

"How will that help me understand what *maya* is?" Narada asks.

Krishna smiles. "Just come. You'll see."

After they have walked for a while, Lord Krishna says, "Narada, I'm thirsty. Fetch me some water to quench my thirst."

Narada goes off in search of water and arrives at a village where a beautiful woman is drawing water from a well. Enchanted by her loveliness, Narada asks for some water. She smiles as she pours water from her jug into his cupped hands and he drinks heartily. Instantly he becomes completely enamored. His mission to fetch water for Krishna recedes like a distant memory. He follows the woman to her home where he meets her father, who is the village chief. Narada immediately asks for the young woman's hand in marriage. The father agrees and the two are married.

Shortly afterward, the father dies and Narada assumes the title and responsibilities of village chief. He and his wife have four beautiful children and many blissful years pass. Then one day, at the peak of Narada's success, a cyclone hits the village, creating thunderstorms and heavy floods. Narada and his family are forced to flee from their home in a boat, but alas, the wind and rain are so severe, the boat capsizes. Narada cannot save his family from drowning. He is cast ashore, where he sobs uncontrollably, grieving over his loss.

In the midst of his sobbing, Narada hears the light and humorous voice of Krishna: "Narada, where were you? It's been more than a half an hour. Where's my water?"

"I just lost my family! Please bring them back to me. I can't live without them!"

"Narada, wake up!" laughs Krishna. "You were dreaming. There were no children. There was no wife. It was all an illusion. This is the power of *maya*—a mirage in the desert that feels so real. Now do you understand?"[44]

In his mind, Narada experienced a waking dream world that felt so real, with a job, home, wife and children.

A slightly different version of the same tale exists in Buddhist literature. The Buddha also taught that the world is an illusion and the wise know this and escape suffering.

In my study and practice of both Eastern and Buddhist teachings, I resisted this idea. How could this world that I could touch, sense and feel be unreal? When my body was in pain, it sure felt very real! My entire medical training aimed to relieve this pain and suffering. Even when I practiced holistic forms of medicine, such as homeopathy, Ayurveda and yoga, my expectation was still the same.

Yet by the time I came to a deep study and practice of ACIM, I had already realized this: all my searching within Western and Eastern medicine as well as complementary and alternative healing arts had not provided answers for permanently relieving my suffering or that of my clients. In my clinical practice, I had often witnessed clients heal from one set of symptoms and then something else would crop up. One client had shared with me how she felt she was always chasing health and it seemed to be just out of her grasp. Slowly I began to understand that these systems of healing I was studying, despite their well-intentioned efforts to heal, were missing something essential: *the need to understand the body in a completely different way.*

What Is the Body?

Quantum mechanics offers another window to this paradox of appearance versus reality. Examine one of your hands. Beneath the skin are superficial tissues that cover muscles, which in turn cover the bones. Yet the bone is also composed of tissues, cells, and ultimately atoms, which contain smaller subatomic particles, such as electrons and protons. At this level we find more space than actual physical matter.

Physicists state that if we were to compare the nucleus or center of an atom with a golf ball, the nearest electron would be about a mile away.[45] This is why physicists agree that atoms consist of about 99.999999999999% space.[46] So, our bodies and all physical objects are 99.999999999999% space!

In the words of Deepak Chopra, MD, we can view the body with the wonder and awe that we might feel when gazing at a starry night:

> If you look at anything physical, you find out that at the quantum level, it is non-physical. The body is made up of atoms and subatomic particles that are moving at lightning speed around huge empty spaces and the body gives off fluctuations of energy and information in a huge void, so essentially your body is proportionately as void as intergalactic space, made out of nothing, but the nothing is actually the source of information and energy.[47]

Albert Einstein also described this "source of information and energy"[48] as a field where the "matter which we perceive is merely nothing but a great concentration of energy in very small regions."[49] Einstein further emphasized the field's role in shaping the universe: "There (is) no place, in our new physics, for both field and matter, field being the only reality."[50]

Now, let's shift gears one moment and look to the Indian spiritual tradition. One of my teachers of meditation and yoga, Swami Rama, shares this profound truth that is a fundamental teaching of the Hindu spiritual tradition:

> The sun, the moon, the stars, and all the lights that you can imagine in the entire external world are but fragments of that one great Light that is within you. It

is the light of knowledge, the light of discrimination, the light of understanding, the light of life, the light of sharing and love, the light of Being that you are.[51]

We can find a similar reference to this field of energy and light in ACIM:

Beyond the body, beyond the sun and stars, past everything you see and yet somehow familiar, is an arc of golden light that stretches as you look into a great and shining circle. And all the circle fills with light before your eyes. The edges of the circle disappear, and what is in it is no longer contained at all. The light expands and covers everything, extending to infinity forever shining and with no break or limit anywhere. Within it everything is joined in perfect continuity. Nor is it possible to imagine that anything could be outside, for there is nowhere that this light is not.

When I first read this, I was awed by the beauty and poetry of these words. Yet I felt a deep ache and longing as well. How is it possible that from spiritual and quantum science perspectives we are energy and light, yet often we experience ourselves as dark, heavy, sad, anxious, depressed, guilty, unworthy, sick and even dying? Gradually, I realized that the answer lies in our perceptions, which emerge directly from our beliefs. One core belief we all share in some form or another is a belief in our separation from this source of light and love.

The Separation that Never Really Happened

Most scientists today believe in the Big Bang model. From an initial infinitesimal volume even smaller than a pore on your skin, the universe expanded rapidly, much like an inflating balloon carrying matter along with it. Physicists believe that even time began with the Big Bang. Thus, all the space, time, energy, and matter that constitute today's universe originated in the Big Bang.[52]

From a metaphysical perspective, ACIM tells us that in the beginning there was no time, no separation. There was just one mind joined in love and oneness, eternal and changeless. A thought arose about what it would be like to have an experience other than oneness, or an experience of duality where there is *one* and *other*. ACIM refers to this as a ludicrous or "tiny mad" idea. It is tiny because it is inconsequential to the omnipotent divine will and thus has absolutely no effect. It is mad because it is insane.

Think of a cell inside the body imagining what it would be like to travel outside of the body on its own. It would be a ridiculous supposition and we would laugh at this. Similarly, it is not possible that a part of the oneness could somehow split off and suddenly have an independent existence outside of everything, apart from infinity. The Course teaches that the instant this thought arose in the mind, an answer was given in the form of Holy Spirit—the voice for our inner wisdom, or oneness, which said that this separation *did not* and *cannot* occur, as it is impossible.

Yet the mind believed in this thought of separation, took it seriously, and forgot to laugh. Instead of listening to the inner wisdom, the mind listened to the voice of fear, which is the false ego voice of separation. A deep guilt arose at doing the unthinkable and unforgivable—choosing to separate from our Source. Now we really did it! Boy, were we in trouble! We must hide! God would punish us or even kill us if we tried to return.

This contrast from the original state of peace, love, unity and oneness was intolerable. The mind could not stand this, so there was a *metaphysical Big Bang* with a projection of guilt and fear to *mis*create a fragmented world of billions of images and parts. Imagine a drinking glass shattering after it falls on the floor. All the small fragments of the glass appear like separate, isolated pieces. Yet at one time, collectively they formed a single beautiful object with a definite function. Like a hologram, each part of the universe we perceive with our senses still reflects our original fear and guilt. The Course states "the circle of fear lies just below the level the body sees, and seems to be the whole foundation on which the world is based."

How Do We Heal Our Minds from Fear?

We manage or, at best, minimize this fear through many different means: anxiolytic medications for anxiety; antibiotics, antiviral medications, and immunizations against disease-causing bacteria and viruses; imprisonment for criminals that we fear can harm us; elaborate surveillance systems for monitoring terrorist activity, and more. All this, so we may feel safe. Well, at least sort of safe. And yet, does the fear ever leave our minds? As soon as we deal with one worry or threat, another soon appears.

The purpose of this discussion is not for us to stop our medications or release all the prisoners or stop airport security protocols. Rather, we are joining here to go deeper into exposing this state of fear. What lies beneath it? What are the underpinnings?

Amazingly, most of us never question the origins of this fear. In the movie *The Matrix*, Morpheus, a symbol of the inner teacher in our minds, speaks to Theo, who senses that something is not right about this world. He feels this persistent discomfort as a "splinter in the mind" that will not let him rest. Morpheus tells Theo we are all born slaves in bondage to the *matrix*, a prison of the mind that we cannot see, taste, or touch. But the matrix—a world pulled over our eyes that blinds us to the truth—is everywhere. Morpheus then offers Theo the choice between two pills. If Theo takes the blue pill, he will continue to sleep and dream. If he chooses the red pill, he will be shown the truth.

Ultimately, the choice to keep dreaming or awaken from this dream of separation, fear and guilt, is Theo's and ours as well. In the words of Albert Einstein:

> A human being... experiences himself, his thoughts and feelings as something separated from the rest—a kind of optical delusion of his consciousness. This delusion is a kind of prison for us, restricting us to our personal desires and to affection for a few persons nearest to us. Our task must be to free ourselves from this prison by widening our circle of compassion to embrace all living creatures and the whole of nature in its beauty.[53]

Einstein refers to the "optical delusion of consciousness" while ACIM bluntly states that we simply do not see. In the introduction to the Course, we are told from the beginning that "the purpose of the workbook is to train your mind in a systematic way to a different perception of everyone and everything in the world." The Course refers to this as seeing through eyes of Christ, spiritual vision, healed perception, or ultimately, forgiveness.

This is not positive thinking whereby we see the world through rose-colored glasses and ignore suffering and pain. It is a radical forgiveness that awakens our inner spiritual vision. We are willing to fully accept all that we perceive—the so-called good and bad—so we can literally whitewash it with a different purpose, that of healing and restoring our minds and hearts to peace. Can you feel how this acceptance is not about resigning to fate, destiny, or the decrees of karma? From this place of deep surrender, as we open to the mighty purpose of healing, we see beyond appearances, or what one of my spiritual teachers from India refers to as the external packaging, and instead, witness the underlying true reality of love.

In the following two chapters, we explore more deeply this idea of radical forgiveness and how it is essential for our healing, regardless of the nature of the problem we may be facing.

CHAPTER 5

Radical Forgiveness: A Way to Wake Up from the Dream of Separation and Reclaim Our Innocence

Yet forgiveness is the means by which I will recognize my innocence.

While reading the Course sections about our false sense of separation, a song from a 1950s Bollywood movie about awakening floated gently into my awareness. I last heard this song when I was in elementary school. I didn't pay much attention to the lyrics, yet even then I found the song both soothing and haunting. When I watched the movie and heard the song again, I was amazed at how the storyline echoed the Course's teachings about awakening from our dream of separation. The name of the movie fittingly is *Jagte Raho* or *Stay Awake*.

The movie opens with a scene of a young man who leaves his village home in search of a better life in the big city of Bombay, today known as Mumbai. We never learn the name of the man nor the name of his home village. He could be anyone arriving from anywhere, searching for something more. He could be any of us who dreams that we left our home in God, or love, for something else.

According to the Course, this tiny mad idea never really happened. However, our belief in separation is so strong that it buries the memory of our oneness with love. Essentially, this memory is hidden away from our everyday awareness.

After walking some distance, the man feels tired and thirsty. It is nighttime. He stops to drink water from a faucet outside a gated community patrolled by a watchman walking around the perimeter of the community shouting, *"Jagte raho!"* (Stay awake!) to keep potential robbers at bay. The watchman mistakes the man for a thief. Initially, the man protests his innocence but then the spell of fear descends. He runs and hides *as if he really were a thief.* That he did nothing wrong becomes a distant memory covered by thick layers of fear and guilt. Essentially, he forgets his core innocence.

Rarely do we see ourselves or others as innocent. Usually it is quite the opposite. We find faults and shortcomings with everything around us and with ourselves as well. The Course lifts us beyond appearances of the relative reality of good and bad, love and hate, oppressed and oppressor, to a non-dualistic view of who we truly are—whole, innocent and complete: changeless and timeless. Krishna, in the *Bhagavad Gita*, more than 2000 years ago, referred to this as Atman or soul:

Know this Atman
Unborn, undying,
Never ceasing,
Never beginning,
Deathless, birthless,
Unchanging forever.
....
Not wounded by weapons,
Not burned by fire,
Not dried by the wind,
Not wetted by water:
Such is the Atman.[54]

The Course awakens the memory of our core innocence through a path of forgiveness. This is not an ethical or moral forgiveness where we forgive but find it difficult if not impossible to forget. Rather, it is a radical forgiveness—a complete washing away of the false sense of who we think we are and who we perceive others to be—limited, flawed and imperfect beings that need to be fixed, changed and improved. The Course is not a curriculum in self-improvement but rather a call to Self-remembrance: the Self that is pure, whole and innocent. The Self that needs no fixing but simply awaits patiently our welcome and acceptance.

Forgetting that he is innocent, the man secretly enters other apartments in the building through terrace doors and open windows to escape from the mob that has gathered and is chasing him while shouting, *"Chor, chor!"* (Thief, thief!) Meanwhile, he witnesses many other robberies: a man stealing golden bracelets from his sleeping wife to pawn for gambling money; a young woman in a clandestine affair with her lover; another home in which, beneath the façade of a respectable business, the owners operate a counterfeit money factory. The Course teaches that the world we perceive is the world of our beliefs. The man truly believes himself to be a thief. Thus, all around him he sees more images of stealing, betrayal and robbery.

Ultimately, the man seeks safety inside an apartment flat that he enters through open balcony doors.[55] There he meets a young girl with curly black hair wearing a white flowing gown. Hastily he closes the doors behind him.

The girl quickly runs and pushes the doors open. "You should keep the door open in the morning. How else will light enter?"

The man pauses. He seems to remember that perhaps this night has all been a bad dream. The morning is here and it's time to wake up.

The girl studies him carefully.

"Are you a thief?" she asks, her wide-eyed expression a mixture of wonderment and amusement.

The man falls exhausted to his knees in front of her. "Little girl, I've done nothing wrong. I'm not a thief. I've done nothing wrong!" He breaks down, sobbing in despair.

In the background, we hear the mob and their shouts of "Chor, chor!" The girl gently wipes the man's tears away and helps him to his feet. The mob could enter any minute from the balcony door. She runs and opens the front door, motioning for the man to leave. The man walks with hesitation and stops at the door, turning to search her eyes as if for a final reassurance.

"Are you afraid?" she asks. "But you've done nothing at all."

The man smiles almost sheepishly. He just needed to be reminded. He makes his exit. Outside, the mob swells with policemen who arrive to investigate. The man is oblivious and walks past the commotion as if it is not even a part of his awareness.

As the Course teaches, we are like little children groping in the dark, mistaking curtains for ghosts, and shadows for dragons. But once we are willing to accept into our minds the light of the inner guide (represented in this movie by the little child), we are no longer afraid. As the night recedes in the light of the morning, finally we awaken from the slumber of darkness inside our minds.

The man now walks confidently and with conviction. His destination is certain. Nothing can harm him or prevent him from reaching his goal. Soon he arrives at a beautiful garden where a woman is singing a prayer of awakening while watering the plants and flowers:

> *The one who lights the lamp of their mind*
> *Will behold a world that is radiant and shining.*
> *Do not depend on your physical eyes.*
> *Arise, wake up![56]*

The woman sees the man and for a moment seems alarmed at the sight of his disheveled appearance. Then a smile spreads slowly across her face and she approaches him. He stretches out his cupped hands, and she pours the water. There are no threatening mobs, no chasing policemen, no angry shouts. The dream of separation is finally over. At last the man's thirst is quenched and he drinks in peace.

A change in mind *can* change everything. This is the message of the Course. It is so simple, we risk dismissing it because of its simplicity. As Mooji, a contemporary spiritual teacher of Advaita or non-dualistic philosophy teaches, the truth is simple, yet the person walking to this truth is complex indeed! To reach that place of stillness where we can feel our core innocence, we must dive beneath all the tangled and twisted cobwebs of confusion within our minds. Like the ocean, the untrained mind is very unsteady with waves of thoughts constantly rolling back and forth. At times it can be like a raging, tumultuous storm. But as we go deeper within the ocean, we find stillness and peace.

To fully experience the peace that resides deep within our minds, we must be willing to go on an archeological mind dig, where we expose all the emotions, thoughts, and beliefs that lie deep within the subconscious mind. We don't do this to figure things out or for more self-analysis. The Course teaches that the ego loves to study itself, but self-analysis does not constitute healing. In fact, although self-analysis can certainly be a helpful first step, if we stop there, often we can get stuck in stories of self-blame or blame projected onto others. Instead, the Course offers a radical form of spiritual psychotherapy whereby we go within for the sole purpose of bringing to the light all our false ideas about ourselves and the world, so they can be healed. This is the essence of forgiveness. At times, like the healing exchange that happened for the man in the movie once he met the young girl, this can happen in an instant. We join with another who mirrors to us our core innocence from which we feel disconnected. However, often it can take time and daily practice.

In the next chapter, we explore a path of radical forgiveness derived from the Hawaiian tradition.

PART TWO

What Are the Dynamics of Healing?

CHAPTER 6

The Ho'oponopono Story: A Demonstration of the Power of Forgiveness

Forgiveness is the key to happiness.

Imagine if your doctor could offer you a medicine that would give you the following:

- Steady and consistent peace of mind
- Happiness that fills you from within, simply bubbles over, and is easily shared with others
- A quiet mind that cannot be disturbed
- A sense of deep, abiding rest and comfort
- Feeling cared for, safe, and protected—always—*no matter what*
- A sense of self-worth and beauty that does not depend on anything external
- An ability to be gentle yet never feel hurt
- A certainty of purpose in a world that often seems senseless and meaningless

All you needed to do was take the medicine daily, perhaps even use it several times a day, if necessary. What if you were also assured that this medication caused absolutely no side effects and there were no interactions with other medications you might be using?

What would you do?

Most, if not all of us, would say, yes, of course, we would happily take the medicine! And now, what if I were to tell you that *forgiveness* is that medicine? Forgiveness, a priceless gift from the beloved presence dwelling within our hearts, is like a soothing balm for healing all our wounds. We need this comforting presence to dry all our tears. Whenever we feel lost, confused, lonely, upset or disconnected, a steady practice of forgiveness anchors us in the truth of our being—a changeless, timeless, deathless, and birthless reality that is pure peace, love, and joy. In our fast-paced lives mired in space, time, and form where the only thing that is constant is change, we are apt to quickly forget this reality.

How Does Forgiveness Help Us Heal?

For me, the practice of radical forgiveness is a deeply transformative process that allows us to experience everything and everyone in a new and fresh way. Forgiveness is not a superficial turning the cheek or pardoning the sins of others. It is not about overlooking some wrongdoing from the past that either we did to someone or someone else did to us.

In truth, we are already perfect, whole, complete, and innocent, so there is nothing to forgive. Yet we cling tenaciously to our false beliefs in lack, scarcity, unworthiness, blame, guilt, and punishment.

I have heard many teachers say that all forgiveness is truly self-forgiveness—a deep washing away of how we see ourselves in relation to our world. I believe we all need forgiveness with the same urgency that a drowning man needs air, or that someone hemorrhaging after a traumatic accident needs a blood transfusion. Often, however, we are not even aware of this need—and even if we were, we may not know how to incorporate a steady practice of forgiveness into our daily lives.

The medicine of forgiveness allows us to see perceived wrongdoing through the eyes of love and compassion, but this doesn't mean we have to forgive everything and everyone overnight. For most of us, it doesn't seem to happen this way. Rather, at a speed and pace that works for us, we decide to see each situation and person differently. In some cases, all we need is an instant and we feel a lifting of the burden of the past as we meet the present without any taint or residue from previous experiences of resentment or anger. Yet at other times, like a savory stew that requires slow cooking for all the ingredients to come together, forgiveness takes time. It is not done until it's done. The speed is inconsequential. What is important is that we clearly understand the value of forgiveness and that we desire it wholeheartedly.

As you are reading this, you might be thinking, "This all sounds marvelous and wonderful, but how does radical forgiveness really work? *How* do we forgive? *What* are we forgiving?" And that, my friend, is exactly the purpose of this chapter—to offer you a systematic practice of forgiveness based on a powerful true story.

A Demonstration of the Healing that Forgiveness Offers

Ho'oponopono [pronounced ho-o-**pono**-pono] is an ancient Hawaiian practice of reconciliation and forgiveness.[57] It means to make right or to correct an error. According to the Hawaiian tradition, painful memories from the past color and cloud our thoughts and this creates errors in our thinking. The practice of Ho'oponopono offers a way for us to literally wash or clean away these memories so we see the world clearly.

From the perspective of ACIM, using Ho'oponopono helps us to see ourselves and the world with a healed perception, or through the eyes of love instead of looking at the world through a dark lens that creates a distorted perception. Before explaining the actual practice of Ho'oponopono, allow me to share the amazing story of Dr. Ihaleakala Hew Len, a psychologist who applied this practice with miraculous results while employed at the Hawaii State Hospital.

Dr. Len worked from 1984 to 1987 in a high security unit for male patients who had committed criminal acts of murder, rape, drug use, and assault and battery against people and property. When Dr. Len arrived at the hospital, it was a dangerous place to work. All the seclusion rooms were occupied with violent patients. Several patients wore metal ankle and wrist restraints to prevent violence—a common occurrence not only by patients against staff but also among the patients themselves. The attendants and doctors working in the ward walked with their backs against the wall, afraid of being attacked by patients. Staff sick leave was also extremely high.

Remarkably, during this time, Dr. Len didn't do any therapy or counseling with the patients. When Dr. Len reviewed the patients' charts, he watched his mind for reactions of repulsion toward the patients, or any feelings of pain within himself. *Instead of trying to change the patients, he worked on himself*, using the Ho'oponopono prayer to clear and heal his feelings and reactions. He repeated this process each time before, during and after leaving the unit. As he continued this ritual, he started to witness change among the patients.

After a few months, shackled patients could walk freely and those requiring heavy medications were able to taper off their dosages. Some patients were even released from the facility. Staff absenteeism was reduced as employees began to enjoy coming to work. Soon there were more staff members than needed because 28 of the 30 patients were released and the remaining two were transferred to another facility. Eventually, the ward was shut down.

Understanding the Practice and Applying It to Our Daily Lives

The updated Ho'oponopono process was not created by Dr. Hew Len but attributed to his teacher, Morrnah Nalamaku Simeona, a *kahuna* (traditional Hawaiian spiritual leader and shaman) who taught him this method in November of 1982. According to Morrnah, each of us is a product of our past experiences. Somewhere within our consciousness, we still carry a burden from our past.[58] Whenever we experience stress, discomfort or any fear in our lives, we react not to the present event but to a memory of a past hurt or wound that is superimposed on the current situation. But because this memory is stored in the subconscious, we continue to believe our upset is caused by the present situation.

In the traditional Ho'oponopono practice, a moderator officiated and facilitated the healing process and the patient's entire family was required to attend. Morrnah transformed the forgiveness process so it became an inside job, making it possible for anyone to practice Ho'oponopono without the need to have a family gathering.

The process of forgiveness that Morrnah shared with Dr. Len, which he then applied in the psychiatric ward, is a simple and beautiful prayer of the heart to restore our minds to our original state of love, peace, and joy. We ask for a healing of all the thoughts and beliefs that seem to be holding us back from connecting to that "zero state" where there are zero limits.[59] From this space, anything is possible and miracles can occur, as they did around Dr. Len.

Briefly, the three parts of this forgiveness process are:

- Repentance (we acknowledge our reactions and whatever feelings may be coming up for us in whatever situation we are facing, whether it is within ourselves or in our family, community, or society at large)

- Asking for forgiveness (for holding the false beliefs that prevent us from seeing our true Self in ourselves or others)

- Transmutation (we ask love, or the divine, to heal our upsetting feelings, emotions, beliefs and memories)

The actual Ho'oponopono prayer used by Dr. Len involves four phrases:

- ▸ I'm sorry
- ▸ Please forgive me
- ▸ Thank you
- ▸ I love you

Let us look at each of these phrases separately, drawing from the radical forgiveness shared by ACIM.

I'm sorry

I am sorry that I do not see our true Self—the place of love and light, of purity and innocence. I accept responsibility for the error that lies in my perception.

Please forgive me

I seek forgiveness for the mistakes in my perception whenever I see lack, guilt, powerlessness, pain, fear, or unworthiness in myself or others.

Now, let's consider application of this part of the Ho'oponopono process. Most of us would agree that if we did say or do something unkind toward another, then being able to say we're sorry or ask for forgiveness would feel helpful and even therapeutic. We would feel less burdened and the other person whom we might have hurt would feel a sense of healing as well. But what if we are the ones experiencing emotional and/or physical pain? Or, what if someone else in our family or community is suffering? How would we then apply this prayer? What have we done for which we need to say we're sorry or ask for forgiveness?

According to Dr. Hew Len,

> The purpose of life is to be restored back to Love, moment to moment. To fulfill this purpose, the individual must acknowledge that he is 100% responsible for creating his life the way it is. He must come to see that it is his thoughts that create his life the way it is moment to moment. The problem is not people, places, and situations but rather thoughts of them. He must come to appreciate that there is no such thing as "out there."[60]

This is exactly in alignment with what we learn in ACIM:

*I **am** responsible for what I see. I choose the feelings I experience, and I decide upon the goal I would achieve. And everything that seems to happen to me I ask for, and receive as I have asked.*

Let's look at this from a scientific perspective. I love when we can find scientific support for what may seem like New Age pop lit. Peter Russell, a British scientist with an extensive background in physics, psychology, and meditation and who serves on the faculty at the Institute of Noetic Sciences, points out that what is outside us is really a reflection or interpretation that we make in our minds, based on past experiences. When we look at an object like a tree, for example, we believe we are seeing the tree directly. Yet when the light enters our eyes, it triggers chemical reactions in the retina. This in turn produces electro-chemical impulses which then reach the brain through nerve fibers. The brain analyzes and interprets these signals and creates its own picture of what seems to be out there. We then have an experience of seeing a tree. However, in truth, we are not really seeing the tree at all but only an image inside our minds. Russell further states that this phenomenon is true of everything we experience. It includes music, color, and even the fragrance of a rose:[61,62]

Dr. Russell states:

> Everything we know, perceive, and imagine, every color, sound, sensation, every thought and every feeling, is a form appearing in the mind. It is all an informing of consciousness.[63]

I have discovered that in my own life and in my coaching practice this concept of taking responsibility for what we see outside of ourselves can be a difficult one to understand and even trickier to apply. Let's turn once more to Dr. Len. When he was working at the hospital psychiatric unit, he would review the charts of the patients and observe his mind for all the judgments, ideas, and beliefs he held about them. He did not engage in any sort of intellectual theorization of why these patients were acting and behaving the way they were or even what should be done differently in terms of treatment. He did not try to change them. He took 100% responsibility for his judgments, opinions, and interpretations, essentially his overall perceptions about these patients, inside his own mind.

It is important to realize that taking responsibility is not about our feeling guilty or holding ourselves as somehow bad or wrong for what is going on around us. This can be a very common misuse of these ideas, which prevents our healing. *We are not taking responsibility for the form of what we see, but rather, for the content of our mind.* Dr. Len did not hold himself guilty for the actions of the prisoners. Yet he did not turn away from them in separation or judgment, but instead, joined with them by using the prayer repeatedly as a bridge. Dr. Len demonstrated how to become a master alchemist, one who can transmute heavy energies of judgment and resistance toward oneself or another into the light of love.

We can apply this prayer to ourselves as well, whenever we are holding ourselves in a space of self-blame, judgment, or guilt. When we say, "I'm sorry," or "Please forgive me," we are essentially asking for forgiveness of ourselves (or a washing or clearing away) of all our interpretations, reactions, and self-judgments. Forgiveness is spiritual alchemy that transforms our mind. It offers us a way to neutralize the energies of our judgments and re-set our minds to a state of being open, empty, and clear—a blank slate. Into this empty space, the love and light that was there all along but merely covered with layers of fear and judgment can shine through.

Thank you

Thank you for the opportunity to become aware of the errors in my perception. Thank you for being the catalyst for my reaching more deeply into my mind beneath the surface of fear and lack to the place of healing and wholeness.

With the third phrase of the Ho'oponopono prayer, we affirm our gratitude for each of our experiences. We clearly understand that everything and everyone in our life provides us with an opportunity for deep healing. In the words of the great Sufi poet Rumi, we treat our life as a "guest house." [64] We learn to welcome everything as it comes, however undesirable or unappealing it may seem to be on the surface. Even if our challenges "violently sweep" the landmarks of our life as we know it, we can make a choice to see it differently. We make a conscious decision to give this challenge the healing purpose of acting as a "guide from beyond" to "clear (us) for some new delight." [65]

I love you

Only love is real and all else is false. Inner light, please shine brightly inside me and clear away all darkness and ignorance inside my mind so I may see everyone and everything through the eyes of love and light.

Love is the true healer. Love leads the way. As the beautiful prayer from Corinthians reminds us, "Three things will last forever—faith, hope, and love—and the greatest of these is love." [66] We are not responsible for healing or fixing anyone or anything. We simply surrender and allow the inner teacher within our hearts to step forth and do the rest. Often, we may receive inner guidance about some inspired action from our inner wisdom to support our healing or that of another.

Perhaps we feel prompted to call a friend, go for a walk, watch a movie, or work with a health care practitioner if we are dealing with an illness. Yet all of this will emerge naturally, just by our being present to our inner wisdom and acting as it feels inspired moment-to-moment and day-to-day.

We Are One

In the movie, *Little Buddha*, there is a beautiful scene that underscores the power of the Ho'oponopono prayer. It offers us a way to join with others facing challenges rather than looking away in avoidance from a stance of separation.[67] Prince Siddhartha Gautama, who will later be known as the Buddha, has lived a sheltered life inside his father's kingdom since his birth. One day, he asks his charioteer to take him outside the palace. For the first time, the young prince witnesses suffering in the form of old age, sickness, and death. He realizes that neither his wealth nor his palatial comforts can protect him or his family from this suffering. During this scene, the prince sheds tears before a burning funeral pyre because he realizes that the suffering of everyone is truly his own. There is no separation. There is no difference.

The Ho'oponopono prayer can empower us. Instead of feeling paralyzed or overwhelmed by our emotions when we witness suffering in our family, larger community, or even in the world, we can use this practice. As we receive healing of our perceptions, we behold a different world. In the healing of others, we find our own healing as well.

Summary

Let's review the process once again:

- We take responsibility for all our interpretations, reactions, and judgments about whatever we perceive and experience (in ourselves or others around us)

- We express that we are sorry and ask for forgiveness (of ourselves or another, or both)

- We express our gratitude for this opportunity for our healing and for the healing of the whole

- Then we simply say, "I love you."

The Ho'oponopono prayer is an effective way to stop the monkey-mind and ask for forgiveness and correction of our thoughts in that moment. It is a form of mental cleansing that allows us to regain our inner balance. From that place, the most helpful action and words seem to flow naturally. It is an easy practice we can do anywhere and anytime. The other person need not be involved. All that is required is our willingness to change our minds with a sincere desire for peace. I invite you to explore this practice and see what you discover.

Without a clear desire for healing, we can accomplish nothing. In the following chapter, we explore the power of this healing desire.

CHAPTER 7

Perception: A Reflection of Our Desire

There is another way of looking at the world.

In the last chapter, we explored in depth the process of radical forgiveness. However, before we can forgive, we must feel a desire to forgive. This is key to healing since nothing happens without our desire. In this chapter, I want to share a story that beautifully illustrates the power of desire in healing a condition that many would see as hopeless.

In his book, *The Brain that Changes Itself*, Dr. Norman Doidge writes about Catalan poet and scholar Pedro Bach-y-Rita and his remarkable recovery from a disabling stroke.[68] I was so inspired by the story, I wanted to know more. Fortunately, I was able to interview Pedro's son, Dr. George Bach-y-Rita, a psychiatrist practicing in San Francisco. Below is a recap of this inspiring story of healing, based on Dr. Doidge's book and my interview with Dr. George.

In 1959 at the age of 65, Pedro, a widower and professor teaching in New York City, suffered a stroke that left him with half his body paralyzed and unable to speak. The doctors did not anticipate any recovery and recommended placement in an institution. George was then a medical student in Mexico. International phone calls were rare in Mexico and usually meant bad news. After receiving the news about his father, George boarded a plane for the very first time and arrived in New York City. There he found his dad, previously a high functioning professor, drooling in a wheelchair.

But Pedro's desire for life remained strong.

"This won't do. This won't do," Pedro repeated.

George visited his kindergarten schoolteacher who was also hospitalized after experiencing a stroke. However, there was a dramatic difference between Pedro and this woman, even if their bodies were affected similarly. Pedro chose life while the schoolteacher did not hope for any possibility of recovery. She died shortly afterward.

George brought his father back to Mexico to live with him. Initially, Pedro completed twelve weeks of outpatient rehabilitation at the American British Hospital and was then sent home without any further treatment options. However, Pedro remained dependent on others for all activities of daily living, including going to the toilet and showering.

Again, Pedro was adamant, *"This won't do."*

In our interview, Dr. George mentioned his papa repeating these words often. Just a few simple words, but they contained a seed of hope that served to propel father and son forward.

George knew nothing about rehabilitation. In hindsight, not knowing was a blessing. Thus, George had the gift of an open mind and drew from the only model he knew—that of watching babies learn. For many months, with help from their gardener, Pedro first learned to crawl with kneepads on all fours. Pedro did this by leaning his weak shoulder and arm against the wall, which became his support. To keep him occupied, George devised games to play together, such as marbles, or having Pedro pick up coins with the weak hand.

The neighbors were appalled at this state of affairs. How could the Professor (as they referred to Pedro) be allowed to crawl on the floor? *This was no way for a son to treat his papa! The Professor should have rest and be cared for properly, not humiliated by crawling around on the floor.* This was the neighbors' perception. Yet George could see that crawling gave his papa a taste of freedom and independence, however small.

George knew his papa enjoyed cooking. After his wife passed away, Pedro assumed responsibility for preparing the family meals. Normal daily activities, like washing pots, now became rehabilitative exercises. Pedro held the pot with his good hand, making his weak hand go round and around the pot for fifteen minutes first clockwise, then fifteen minutes counterclockwise. Gradually, his spastic, jerky and uncontrolled motions became precise and smooth, using the inside limited circumference of the pot to contain the weak hand.

After several months of daily exercises lasting many hours a day, Pedro went from crawling on all fours to moving on his knees to standing and finally to walking. Pedro struggled with his speech but within a few months this also began to return. Then he wanted to resume writing. To do this, Pedro sat in front of the typewriter, first hitting the keys by dropping his whole arm, then gradually using just the wrist, then the fingers. Pedro never regained complete control of his right hand as he had before. Rather than use all five fingers of the hand, he had to type using two fingers. But this did not stop him.

Remarkably, just after one year, Pedro returned to full-time teaching at City College in New York City. He worked until he retired at age 70 and remarried after meeting his future wife at a concert at Carnegie Hall in New York. They moved to San Francisco where Pedro continued to teach, work, hike and travel. At the age of 73, while hiking with friends at an altitude of 9,000 feet in the mountains of Columbia, he suffered a heart attack. Some weeks later he died.

In his book, Dr. Doidge shares how Pedro's body was brought to San Francisco, where his other son, Paul Bach-y-Rita, was working as a physician researcher. This was the mid-1960s when there were no CT or MRI scans. Often an autopsy was performed to allow doctors to learn more about brain disease and why a patient died.

The autopsy revealed a huge lesion in Pedro's brain that had never healed. The damage was catastrophic—94% of the motor tract nerves that run from the cerebral cortex to the spinal cord were destroyed. Yet Pedro had recovered, despite this extreme damage!

Paul was stunned. Gradually, he realized this must have occurred due to the extensive rehabilitative work his papa did with George. Pedro's brain had reorganized itself *without the use of medications or surgery*. Areas of the brain had started doing the work of the damaged areas. Pedro's was the first published case of neuroplasticity in an adult brain that was confirmed by histopathology.

Paul changed his career path after his papa's death when he recognized the significance of what he had seen. In his forties, he went from working primarily as a researcher in eye muscle pathology to training in neurology and rehabilitation, so he could re-create the miracle he had witnessed with his father.

Paul made pioneering contributions to the field of neuroplasticity. He passed away in 2006.

The Power of Making a Decision for Healing

The basic premise of neuroplasticity—that the brain can change itself without surgery or drugs—is certainly groundbreaking. It dispels much of what I had learned about the brain when I was in medical school. For example, I learned that if the cells of the brain were injured or failed to develop properly, then their function could not be replaced. Pedro's case, however, and so many other similar ones in the field of neuroplasticity now prove that the brain has an innate capacity to heal by using other areas to perform functions that were once managed by those areas that are now dead. This is certainly remarkable and miraculous.

However, in first learning about Pedro's story, I was most impressed by how a simple change of perception can heal. Dr. George also felt strongly that his father's attitude was central to his healing.

When Pedro said, *"This won't do,"* he expressed a firm decision in the mind not to accept his current very limited physical state as a final decree of fate or a permanent result of his stroke. His words portended a sense that this was not where his life would end. There was still more.

Dr. George and his father did not have any knowledge about rehabilitation and there were no imaging studies. In hindsight, these were fortunate occurrences. This allowed the mind to be open, and from this spaciousness arose a new and fresh way to see Papa. He was not a poor, disabled and crippled professor as seen by the other doctors in New York City or the neighbors in Mexico. Instead, he was an infant who just needed to learn everything all over again, with patience and love.

Dr. George shared how he and his dad moved through life at that time by taking baby steps, literally and metaphorically. Pedro's body transformed, reflecting a decision for healing made *first within the mind.* Just like babies when first learning to walk fall countless times yet never doubt their innate capacity for walking, so a mind that wants healing must choose love and life again and again, regardless of what the body's eyes seem to report. Pedro's decision to choose life and healing while his body experienced profound disability and paralysis was the *real* miracle. Apparently, Dr. George's kindergarten teacher was not able to choose similarly.

Levels of Mind: Connecting with Our Desire

To go a bit deeper with what happens in the mind based on our decision for healing, I would like to share a diagram created by David Hoffmeister, a teacher of *A Course in Miracles.*[69]

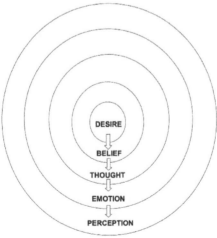

THE LAYERS OF MIND THAT FORM PERCEPTION

The Course teaches that it is *our* choice regarding what we want to see that determines what we do see. My perception of the world I see is determined by my emotions, which come from my thoughts, which stem from my beliefs. At the center is my desire. What I find very instructive about this diagram is that the arrow points from desire outward to perception. It is not my perception—which is just my interpretation of events—that determines my experience. Rather, it is my desire. What do I truly want to experience? This ultimately defines my perception. As Gerald Jampolsky, MD, a child and adult psychiatrist and beloved veteran teacher of *A Course in Miracles,* often says: you can either be a fault-finder or a love-finder. The choice is yours.[70]

In September of 1929, Pedro became tenured as a professor at City College in New York City. Next month the stock market crashed, and he and the other professors were asked to work as long as they could without pay because of the financial crisis. Instead of seeing this as a catastrophe, Pedro and his wife chose to board third class on a steamer ship to Europe, where he could complete his PhD thesis. For the next few years, the young couple enjoyed their lives in Europe while Pedro completed his thesis in literature with access to the best libraries in the world. Although he had no control over the economic climate, Pedro aligned with the only choice he had—the only choice any one of us have. How do I choose to perceive this situation?

As the Course teaches, beneath all seeming problems lies a choice always between love and fear. Our experience of ourselves and the world we perceive rests upon our choice. If we have chosen fear, doubt, or a grievance, we can even bring Pedro's words to mind: *"This won't do. This won't do."* And, we *can* choose again. From our new choice, the actions that would be most helpful to remedy our pain and suffering can emerge as well—as they did for Pedro and George.

In the next three chapters, I share my journey of healing with my own papa. Like Pedro and George, my papa and I also needed to choose—again and again—love over fear, and at times, even life over death.

CHAPTER 8

Listening to the Voice for God

The Voice of the Holy Spirit does not command, because It is incapable of arrogance. It does not demand, because It does not seek control... It merely reminds. It is compelling only because of what It reminds you of. It brings to your mind the other way, remaining quiet even in the midst of the turmoil you may make. The Voice for God is always quiet, because It speaks of peace.

For as long as I can recall, I have been plagued by a terror of death—not so much my own death, but the death of my family members, especially my parents. Perhaps that is what propelled me, at least unconsciously, to a career in medicine. Studies indicate that doctors have an above-average fear of death.[71] Perhaps we enter medicine to work through our fears.

During my childhood and adolescent years, I dreamed of my father being killed. The scenario varied; sometimes he was stabbed, other times he was shot dead. It was always violent and I would wake up sobbing. I found an outlet during college, writing term papers for my classes in psychology and sociology on death and dying. In the basement floor of the library at City College in New York City, before the era of the digital world, I eagerly photocopied articles from the *Journal of Thanatology*. I was thrilled to find that such a journal even existed. Apparently, I wasn't the only one who was both fascinated *and* repelled by death.

As a first-year medical student in July 1988, like most of my fellow students, I was less concerned with working through my fears and more focused on not flunking Anatomy. For me, the challenge was more than just the academics. From the first moment I set foot in the Anatomy lab, I hated it. It was not a simple distaste. It was a visceral repulsion, like food poisoning. Here, however, there was no relief in the form of vomiting or diarrhea. I would shower each morning and again each evening, but I never felt clean. The smell of formaldehyde passed through my clothes to my skin and clung to my very being like industrial smog that hangs over cities in the summer air. The sight of the cadaver. The dissection of the skin, the tissues, the organs. Memorizing and identifying all the different organ parts, the muscles and nerves and vessels. Everything sickened me.

According to *A Course in Miracles*, death is not just the passing of the physical body, but rather, it is any ego mind-based thought of sadness, fear, anxiety, or doubt. The ego mind is literally a death wish. Whenever we forget that at our core we are blessed with an unlimited reservoir of light, energy, and bliss, this death wish creeps into our minds. Certainly, that summer I felt death within me and saw it outside as well. I felt a gnawing uncertainty and at times a profound sadness that the path of medicine was perhaps not the path of my heart. Today I realize that the cadavers simply reflected the death and dying within myself.

That July, on the day before my 21st birthday and during the hottest part of the day, try as I might, I could not force myself to focus any longer on the *Gray's Anatomy* textbook before me. I was sitting on the back porch of my parents' home in Queens, New York, facing the garden. It felt less painful to study Anatomy among the beauty of pink, violet, and red impatiens and vibrant orange marigolds. How alive everything was! How could a dead cadaver teach me about life and healing? It didn't make any sense. With a heavy sigh, I closed the book and decided to take a nap. My sleep was restless. I dreamed of hearing the shrill cry of an ambulance racing to help someone in need.

Soon I was awakened by yet another piercing sound. It was my mom on the phone. Her voice was strained; instantly I knew something was wrong. They were shopping at the market... A man with a gun had shot Papa... They were at the hospital... I must come right away. Let Guruji,[72] our spiritual teacher, know... Then her voice dissolved into muffled sobs... *I must come right away...*

I found Papa in one of the trauma beds in the ER. The bullet had entered the left side of his chest. Luckily it had just missed his heart but caused much injury to his lungs and some of the other major vessels in his body. He had lost a lot of blood, so his blood pressure was low. He wore an oxygen mask and was getting a blood transfusion. Although Papa could not utter more than single broken words, I recall how his eyes held their usual alertness. They were very much alive, still able to take everything in, not missing a single detail.

My mom sat in a chair next to his bed. She is a petite woman, a few inches short of five feet tall. For many years, she suffered from debilitating anxiety and chronic pain associated with headaches and arthritis. It was my dad who was the strong and healthy one. Often he joked how he never even needed to take Tylenol. But today, the roles were suddenly reversed. Today Mom appeared strangely strong and calm despite the trauma she must have endured in the last few hours.

As soon as I entered the room, Papa's face broke into a huge smile. "Seema…" Just saying my name required tremendous energy.

"How did this all happen, Mom?" I searched her eyes for answers.

Before she could respond, Guruji arrived.

Papa's eyes filled with tears. His broken voice began to chant, "Gu-ru-ji, Gu-ru-ji, Gu-ru-ji…"

We moved to the side as Guruji came to the edge of Papa's bed and reached for his hands.

"Mitra, my dearest Mitra."

Guruji, as my family addressed him, or Sri Chinmoy Kumar Ghose, was originally from India. For the past few decades, he had lived in New York City, where he taught and offered meditation sessions at the United Nations. Guruji had been our spiritual teacher for the past year.

Guruji and Papa's hands interlocked and rested upon Papa's chest for what seemed like an eternity. Guruji's silver hair contrasted with his mostly bald, almond-colored head. His passion for tennis matched that of his devotion to meditation and prayer, and today he was aptly dressed in a striped tennis T-shirt and white shorts.

Guruji bowed forward over Papa, who also closed his eyes and fell silent. They seemed as one, an unbroken circle where giver and receiver merge. Surrounding them, the ER activity proceeded as usual. Typically, the cacophony of the ER was all that one heard—phones ringing, the crying of a child, doctors' voices ordering medications and tests. But today, sounds receded and time stood still. Amidst the hectic pace of the ER, Papa and Guruji created an oasis of peace and serenity. Guruji then gently removed his hands from Papa's chest and brought them together in a prayer pose, bowing deeply. Papa immediately opened his eyes.

"Thank you, Guruji. Thank you, sir."

"Your heart is so pure, so pure. You are receiving all I am bringing. Receiving it all on the strength of your gratitude and willingness."

"Gu-ru-ji, Gu-ru-ji, Gu-ru-ji..." Papa chanted again, his eyes closing.

My mom also closed her eyes in prayer.

"Do not think about the culprit right now," said Guruji. "We must all pray for your father. We must all meditate for him."

He spoke in a soft voice, so we listened attentively amidst the ER noise. "You must also inform all your near and dear ones, here and in India, so they can pray for your father."

Guruji walked slowly toward the door and passed me as I stood in the doorway. I felt the pressure rise in my throat as I struggled to hold back my tears. His eyes met mine and he shook his head gently at me. He held my glance just for a moment, but it was enough.

My tears ceased almost immediately. The sadness evaporated, and peace washed over me. For the first time that summer, I felt alive, like I had finally found my purpose. I was to pray and meditate for Papa. I felt like someone drowning who suddenly finds a life boat to carry them safely ashore.

Joseph Campbell, the renowned scholar of world mythology, once said that he did not believe we're looking for the meaning of life as much as "an experience of being alive, so that our life experiences on the purely physical plane will have resonances with our own innermost being and reality, so that we actually feel the rapture of being alive."[73]

On the surface it appeared that Papa was the one wounded and fighting for his life. Yet as I write this today, it is clear to me that Papa's condition reflected the conflict within my own mind between fear and love, death and life, trust and doubt, as it related to my future career in medicine.

In contrast to the symbols of death and dying, my spiritual teacher was a symbol of the inner guide—the great comforter, the deep inner wisdom—reminding me gently yet firmly of the other way, the way of love, peace and healing.

Do not think of the culprit.
We must all pray for your father.
We must all meditate for him.

As I joined with Guruji in his request for prayer and meditation, I felt my medical school obligation as a student to memorize, perform, and succeed miraculously fall away. It was as if someone had just removed a load of bricks from my shoulders. I felt incredibly light and completely fearless. The ER continued around me with its typical frenetic pace, yet I was now standing in the eye of the storm. Nothing could touch me here.

My medical mind, with its knowledge of anatomy and physiology, understood the gravity of Papa's condition. But somehow, I knew that my papa would be okay. I knew this without the slightest of doubts. And everything else—the thinking mind, the noisy and hectic pace of the ER, the coming and going of the doctors and nurses—all seemed to fade away before this inner knowing. I experienced what

ACIM refers to as the *holy instant* in which we choose to live fully in the present moment, letting all fears of past and future recede.

In my pursuit of a career in medicine, I felt a sense of obligation and pressure but now I felt no urgency, no coercion, no sense of command or demand. In the midst all the chaos and turmoil, it seemed like the most natural thing to do was to become still in prayer and meditation. The only sane choice I *could* make was peace and healing. Little did I realize then that the way I viewed medicine and healing would be fundamentally changed forever.

CHAPTER 9

Training the Mind: Aligning with the Flow of Grace

*Grace is acceptance of the Love of God within a world of
seeming hate and fear. By grace alone the hate and fear are
gone, for grace presents a state so opposite to everything the
world contains, that those whose minds are lighted by the gift of
grace can not believe the world of fear is real.*

"You know your papa never listens." Mom sipped her tea
slowly.

Papa was in the operating room. We sat in the hospital
cafeteria as she recounted the events of the shooting.

Mom didn't want anything to eat. Her solution to every
ailment was tea, or rather, chai with fennel and cardamom.
She always had a pot of boiling spiced chai water ready in her
kitchen. No visitor left our house without being served her
famous chai.

"We finished shopping for vegetables. And it was getting so
hot. Papa was getting all red in his face. I knew he was tired
but still pushing ahead, like always. Always one more thing
to do, one more thing to get."

She shook her head ruefully. Her eyes were dry.

"What more did you need?" I asked.

"The bread for the potato cutlets, to make *prasad*[74] for Guruji
tomorrow for your birthday."

I reflected on the irony of this. My dad was in the operating room fighting for his life and tomorrow was my 21st birthday. According to Indian custom, my mom planned to make snacks for Guruji and his other students for a meditation service. Afterward, I would seek Guruji's blessings. As a small gift in honor of Guruji, I had made a hundred or so bookmarks on colored index cards, with his picture and a gratitude prayer handwritten underneath. These would be presented with the *prasad*.

"I told your father we should go home. I told him, 'I'll fix you lunch, you can take your nap and then we'll come back later when it's cooler,' but he insisted on going to the bakery for the bread."

If only he had listened, maybe this awful misfortune would not have happened. My mind filled with remorse and regret.

"And just as we come out and get to the car, we hear this shouting from the store. A man was running out of the doorway. They told us he robbed the store."

Mom spoke in a very matter-of-fact tone, like a witness simply reporting events. Her calm demeanor surprised me.

"Everything happened so quickly. Suddenly this man is next to Papa. I'm on the other side of the car. I don't even hear anything. Then your Papa is saying, 'He shot me, he shot me!'"

I felt my mind reel as I visualized what my mom just experienced.

"The man was gone, and Papa fell to the floor. I held his head in my lap. His face turned yellow, then white. And all that blood... all the blood..." Mom shook her head as if still in disbelief.

"No one was there to help you? What about the bakery people?" I asked. A sick feeling rose from the pit of my stomach.

"Oh, they were there. One girl called the ambulance. Another brought us water... but the ambulance took forever to come. And it was so hot."

"So, what did you do?"

"I just held his head in my lap. The sun was at its peak. And I thought to myself, how powerful the sun is."

Every morning at home, my mom chanted prayers to the sun, facing eastward. She would fill a small Indian brass copper pot with water and a little milk and sugar and then pour it slowly onto the ground in our garden as an offering of devotion to the sun.

"I prayed to the sun to take care of Papa and to give him strength," she said now.

I listened with amazement. *How did she find the presence of mind to pray and not panic?*

"He was getting weaker and weaker, saying again and again, 'I'm going to die, I'm going to die.' And I would tell him, 'No, just chant Guruji's name.'"

Mom paused to sip her tea and continued, "Then Papa said, 'Gu-ru-ji, Gu-ru-ji, Gu-ru-ji... I'm going to die, I'm going to die.' And I would say, 'No, no, just say Guruji. Just take his name. You're going to be fine.' For once he listened. For once he listened." Her lips turned slightly upwards into a faint smile.

But how did she not think about the man who had caused this awful, horrendous misfortune? How could she not get angry? I was still unable to wrap my head around her response.

"I did think about the man who shot Papa," she continued, as if reading my mind. "But you know, Seema, I didn't feel anger. I thought, 'He's ruined my family, but God give him wisdom not to hurt anyone else.' And I just prayed and chanted Guruji's name."

Guruji later told us that grace had surrounded Papa and our family since the beginning of the incident. The Course says that "grace is the acceptance of the Love of God within a world of seeming hate and fear."

Grace is a gift received freely when we choose miracle-mindedness (the voice for love and peace) rather than listening to the sleeping or the unaware mind (the voice of ego, fear, and separation). By chanting the name of our external teacher, or Guruji, my mom aligned with the inner teacher and dipped into the river of grace that is forever and always present. She then invited my dad to join as well, and the miracle flowed forth. She stayed calm and open to love in a condition that was conducive to anything but that. She was even able to bless the man who had just shot her husband before her very own eyes, that he may not harm another. Such an action cannot make any sense from a worldly perspective. It can only be understood from inside the experience of the miracle.

Guruji had taught me my first lesson in mind training when he asked us to not think about what happened or about the person who had harmed Papa but instead spend our time in prayer and meditation. My mom did exactly this, right from the very beginning. The Course teaches that an untrained mind can accomplish nothing. Perhaps the greatest gift we can give to ourselves and the world is a well-trained mind that is in service of love, instead of ego or fear. A well-trained mind consciously chooses to find its way back to peace each time it is aware that peace is lost.

However, this is easier said than done. I recall a story about the Buddha when he returned to his father's palace after attaining enlightenment. His father, who was the king, immediately offered his son rulership over the entire kingdom. The Buddha replied that the greatest victory one can experience in human form is the mastery of one's mind. If one can rule over one's mind, all other autocracies and kingdoms are meaningless.

In ancient India, trainers led elephants across the land and often encountered village bazaars filled with a rich potpourri of sights, tastes, smells, and sounds that easily tantalize and captivate the senses. To prevent the elephants from touching the foods and other items, the trainers placed a wooden stick in their trunks. They were then able to lead the elephants safely through the bazaars.

Our minds also need a stick to keep them focused. Otherwise, our thoughts usually lead us aimlessly in the direction of fear and suffering. In those days, my family and I were introduced to meditation by Guruji. He was our focus and as he entered meditation we would feel peace extending from him. Often meditation seemed to just happen, as if we were carried along the river of peace flowing from our teacher. At other times we recited chants or prayers in praise of different gods and goddesses. Then too, the chanting and music naturally drew us to an experience of peace.

But here in the hospital there was no temple. No altar. No chanting. No music.

One of the hospital nurses led us to a small room off one side of the ER. It was a plain white-painted room used for storage of hospital supplies. In one corner was a table with a few chairs. My mom and I and a few fellow students of Sri Chinmoy sat on the chairs. On the table we placed two small photographs: one of our teacher and one of our family deity, the Goddess Durga, or *Sheron-waali*, "the one who sits upon a lion." We had also requested that a pocket-size photo of Durga and Guruji be near Papa during the operation, and the OR nurse agreed.

In the photo, Durga is portrayed as a beautiful goddess with eight arms, in which she holds a bow and arrow and a sword as well as a lotus flower and a white conch. One of her hands is raised in a pose of *ashirwad*, or blessings. Durga is dressed in a *sari*[75] and resplendent in golden jewelry and a golden crown. A smile plays upon her lips and her eyes convey compassion and serenity. Nothing can disturb her joyful tranquility. Her serene and loving countenance is in stark contrast to the ferocious roar of the lion, her vehicle of transport. As a young girl, I grew up hearing many stories from Indian mythology about Durga taking up arms to protect and defend her devotees.

As soon as I sat in the chair to begin our prayer and meditation vigil, I realized that what I needed most was love—to simply be held in the loving, strong, and compassionate arms of the Goddess. I needed *not* to have to do anything or fix anything or make anything happen. I needed simply to be held in love.

Durga's eyes seemed alive to me. I could hear her comforting me.

All is okay. All is well.
You are not alone.
I've got you all, including your papa.

Just as I had often experienced a flow of peace from my teacher, now I felt a wave of love flow from Durga. I could see a yellow glow emanating from the photograph; it seemed to illumine the entire room. My feet and hands began to feel warm as well. Soon my tears flowed freely, but they were not from fear or sadness. I felt profoundly grateful, and with each tear my heart felt progressively lighter.

During that entire summer while I was studying Anatomy, it was impossible for me to experience even an iota of peace. In fact, I was convinced that finding peace was like looking for a needle in a haystack. But now I felt myself literally swimming in an ocean of peace and love.

On the perceptual level, a tragedy surrounded my family. Yet by joining in prayer and meditation, we connected with the inner teacher, the divine mother/father within us all. Our purpose was simple—a pure desire for peace and healing. Through this profound uniting of minds and hearts, we were carried beyond the world to a state of grace. From this space, the miracle flowed forth. Somewhere in the middle of the night, after almost eight hours of surgery, we received news that Papa had made it through. The next 24 to 48 hours would still be critical but with the grace of the Goddess, he had survived the surgery.

CHAPTER 10

Rising Above the Laws of the World, Resting in Gratitude, and Retreat into Medical School

There are no laws except the laws of God.

It is insane to offer thanks because of suffering. But it is equally insane to fail in gratitude to One Who offers you the certain means whereby all pain is healed, and suffering replaced with laughter and with happiness... Today we learn to think of gratitude in place of anger, malice and revenge.

We first saw Papa after his surgery in the early morning hours. He was sedated and breathing with the help of a respirator. He was also connected to many different intravenous lines supporting him with fluid and medications. I noticed the photos we had provided of Goddess Durga and Guruji were securely attached with white medical dressing tape to one of the IV poles. On the tape in red ink, I read the handwritten words: *Property of patient. Do not remove.*

Papa's shoulders were bare but the rest of his chest, torso and abdomen were completely bandaged. He looked both strong and vulnerable. A solid stillness or a *knowing* seemed to emanate from him and surrounded him. My medical monkey-mind surrendered to this stillness. I was keenly aware the information displayed on the monitors and heard the steady hum of the ventilator as well as the beeping of the various machines. But there was no desire to figure anything out. My only desire was to keep my mind steady and tuned into this flow of peace, which felt like my lifeline — the only *real* thing that sustained me as this surreal experience seemed to play out before me.

With this peace was a profound gratitude for all the doctors, nurses, and other therapists caring for Papa. They seemed to be helpers that were hand-chosen by the universe. Later we learned that the primary surgeon was one of the best trauma surgeons in Queens. The hospital that became our second home that summer was not only minutes away from our house, but also one of the best trauma centers in the area.

My family and I experienced an implicit faith that we were part of a greater plan, like threads in the hands of a master weaver, each thread woven together to create a magnificent tapestry. We could not see the whole; all we could do was simply show up, play our part, and pray and meditate, while the medical staff did their work. Our family expanded to include hundreds of fellow students of Sri Chnimoy. They brought us food and even clothing when we were unable to return home. Many joined us in prayer and meditation — some for hours and even days at a stretch. Thousands of miles away in India, our relatives performed similar prayer vigils.

About 24 hours after the surgery, still breathing with the help of the respirator, Papa "spoke" his first words, written with my mother's help on a writing pad.

"Guruji all for us. Guru is for us. Guru for us."

Even before the shooting, Papa's eyes filled with tears of gratitude each time he saw Guruji. During Guruji's visit after Papa was off the respirator, again Papa began to cry.

"Guruji… Oh Guruji…" he chanted. "Oh Guruji, I was gone… I was gone…I was gone. You brought me back. I will never forget this, sir."

"I am nothing, nothing, nothing." Guruji folded his hands in prayer and bowed his head. "Our Beloved Supreme is everything."

"When I was shot, my wife said, 'Just say Guruji, Guruji, Guruji.' You saved me. Thank you! I owe you my life, my family's life."

"I offer you my heart of infinite love. I offer you my blessings of joy and gratitude. Thank you for your life that readily and soulfully responded to God's Omnipotent Will."

"Please, Guruji, I want to touch your hand."

Guruji smiled. "Of course, I will touch your hand. I will touch your heart. You have such a pure, pure heart. My heart is your heart. Your heart is my heart. I am so proud of you. You have been so receptive to the infinite light and blessings from our Beloved Supreme."

"Guruji, I don't know meditation, but I just repeat your name. Again, and again. And I know you're always with me. In my every breath."

"This is the best, best, best, best possible meditation," smiled Guruji.

"I will come and visit you soon, Guruji. I will come soon. Thank you, sir."

Papa's words conveyed his faith in his recovery. Faith even while he was still recuperating in the hospital from massive injuries.

Guruji knew Papa was concerned not just for himself but also his family. He would assure him,

You have no responsibilities whatsoever.
You are a beloved, dear child of God.
He shall be responsible, as He was before, as He is now.
Forever and forever, throughout eternity, He is responsible for you and your dear ones.

And then Guruji would often tell us, "Always think pure thoughts and keep a clear mind. Do not think about the culprit. Do not worry. Focus on your father. And pray and meditate intensely."

It is difficult to convey the state of our minds during those days. It was like being lifted above the laws of the world to a place where there is no worry, no fear, and no future planning. Just showing up. Being present. Being available.

Whatever problems seemed to appear also seemed to vanish or resolve without any effort on our part. For example, before the first surgery we were told Papa would need several units of blood since his blood pressure was low and he had lost a lot of blood. There was no sense of panic or fear, just a simple acceptance and no resistance. At the end of the surgery we learned that to the surprise of the surgeons, only a few units were needed.

Another time, Papa needed a CT scan, yet the hospital machine wasn't working. Papa needed to be transported to a nearby hospital. He was still intubated so this was risky yet necessary. Once more, as we continued our prayer and meditation, we simply listened and trusted in the medical team to do what was needed. A few hours later, we received news that the hospital CT scan machine was fixed and there was no need to transport Papa.

The medical team also was impressed with how calmly we all listened with presence and equanimity to whatever information they gave us, regardless of whether it was negative or positive. Our reference point was not mired in the constantly fluctuating changes inherent to healing of the body but rather rooted steadfastly in an inner knowing, trust, and faith. We were moving about *in* the world of the hospital, doctors, nurses, surgeons, X-rays, CT scans and so forth, but we did not feel like we were *of* this world.

About two weeks after the first surgery, the doctors grew concerned about Papa's persistent fast heart rate and hypertension that were not responding to medical treatment. Numerous tests were ordered but the doctors were stumped. One day the senior trauma surgeon who performed the initial surgery auscultated my dad's lungs and heart from an unusual place on his back. He ordered an aortic angiogram, which confirmed that Papa had an aortocaval fistula.[76] The next day a vascular surgeon spoke to me about a second surgery that was needed, and possible complications that included bleeding, paralysis or even death. I heard exactly what he said, and I understood even more because of my medical studies. Yet I distinctly recall feeling a sense of complete, unwavering faith. I *knew* Papa would be fine. I just knew it.

The surgeon asked me if he should talk to my dad about this.

"No, that's not necessary. Thank you. You've explained this to us. That's enough," I replied with a confidence that surprised me.

My mom was with me and listened to the surgeon, who was from India. She folded her hands in Namaste gesture. "We're both from India. I believe that *Bhagwan*[77] will work through you."

Despite her diminutive, delicate frame, Mom was like a solid rock of unshakeable faith that simply could not be moved. The surgeon looked at her, then at me, and was speechless. Finally he smiled and folded his hands in Namaste greeting and walked silently away.

In those days, I often perceived a scent of incense—a definite aroma of sandalwood. No one else observed this and it was not associated with any particular place. At different times during the day, the smell simply wafted through the air. It was so distinct yet so familiar to me since Papa often brought this type of incense home from our trips to India. He would light it as part of his morning prayers. What a world of difference from earlier in the summer, when all I could smell was formaldehyde!

One memory forever etched in my mind is that of my mother sitting in the hospital chapel, dressed in a traditional rust-colored Punjabi *salwar kameez*,[78] with a red scarf draped over her head, praying almost ceaselessly, often sleeplessly, for Papa's life. At one point, Guruji entered the chapel when visiting the hospital and stood for several moments with his hand placed on her head in blessing. Mom was so absorbed in her meditation that she did not even realize he was there. Later Guruji commented that my mom's devotion was like that of Savitri, a beautiful princess from ancient Indian mythology whose steadfast love for her husband, Satyavan, a handsome prince, forced Yamaraja (the Lord of Death) to restore his life even after his physical death.[79]

About two weeks after his second surgery, I mentioned to Papa how fortunate we were to have Guruji and all our fellow spiritual brothers and sisters by our side. Papa was resting on the hospital bed and he slowly closed his eyes, turning his head slightly from side to side. He took a deep breath, and when he opened his eyes, I could see that they were misted over.

"Guruji saved our family's pride," he said. "He saved our family's existence. Otherwise our family would have been destroyed."

Exactly six weeks after the shooting, Papa was discharged from the hospital. Eleven weeks after the incident, he flew to Texas to complete his work assignment as a contract engineer. All of us, including his doctors and our entire spiritual community both here and in India, were amazed at his recovery.

There is a famous saying in Hindi that even if the entire world should become our enemy, if we are protected by God, not even a single hair on our head can be harmed. Certainly that summer I learned that above all the laws of medicine and surgery are the laws of God; and as the Course teaches, there is "no loss under the laws of God."

That summer, I also managed to survive Anatomy! The night before the final exam, I slept with the Anatomy book under a pillow on one of the hospital couches. I got an A as the questions were the ones my medical school buddies had reviewed with me. As I write this today, I am reminded that when we "let go and let God," every detail is taken care of, even an Anatomy exam.

At different points during our stay, we were approached by a detective assigned to the case to see if my parents could identify the man who had shot Papa, so he could be apprehended. For the most part, we avoided engaging in any conversation with the detective because we were honoring Guruji's guidance to not think about the shooting but instead, focus on Papa's healing and recovery. The detective reluctantly acquiesced and respected our wishes. Eventually, prior to discharge, he approached us again. However, neither Papa nor Mom could recall any identifying details, nor pick him out of many pictures of men convicted of other crimes. To this day, we don't know if the man responsible for the shooting was ever arrested.

Papa's shooting could have been just another mortality statistic reported on the nightly news or presented during hospital grand rounds as a senseless symbol of fear, hatred and violence. Yet with the guidance and support of a spiritual master who saw beyond what seemed to be happening on the physical plane, doctors committed to their craft, and a mighty circle of family and friends joined in prayer and meditation, all the ugliness was washed away. Instead, a lovely vision of healing emerged. Perhaps the glue of it all was gratitude that connected Papa, Guruji, and each of us, breath by breath, moment by moment, in prayer, meditation, and healing.

I wish I could say Papa's miraculous experience healed the split in my mind regarding my medical school career. Or that I felt free to follow my heart and devote my life to a path of spiritual devotion with Guruji as my teacher.

My life was yet to take another turn when Guruji announced he would now teach only those serious spiritual seekers who were willing to observe a vow of life-long celibacy. This vision did not sit right for my family or for myself. Although we felt a deep respect and devotion for Guruji and an undying gratitude for all that he and his students shared, gradually we became less involved with him and his spiritual community.

Unfortunately this left a huge vacuum in my life. I felt like I had lost not only a teacher, guide, and father figure, but also a whole community of spiritual brothers and sisters. My parents took the break more easily than I did. They felt a deep devotion to Guruji inside their hearts and did not feel the need for an ongoing physical connection. For me, the time spent with Guruji and his community was the closest I felt to belonging anywhere in my life.

Now I felt completely abandoned. I was filled with even greater doubt that the world of medicine and spirituality could ever come together for me in my life. I needed to choose. Either way, a sacrifice was demanded. To follow the path of spiritual awakening meant to renounce the worldly life. To follow the path of medicine meant the voice of my deeper inner knowing would need to be ignored.

Predictably, I chose the path of least resistance and once more retreated into the world of medical school. Most of the time I found myself in survival mode, doing my best to stay afloat amidst the discombobulating agenda of countless hours of study, endless litany of tests, and thousands of facts to remember and successfully regurgitate.

Other times I felt inspired to read books about holistic medicine, spirituality and the mental and emotional aspects of healing. I enjoyed attending workshops on these topics and inviting speakers to share these ideas with other students at my medical school. For a while, many different popular New Age authors, including Louise Hay, Shakti Gawain, Deepak Chopra, and others, became my teachers. Their books kept a spark alive somewhere in my mind that there was another dimension to healing that lay beyond the daily limited worldview presented in medical school.

CHAPTER 11

I Am Not a Body. I Am Free. For I Am Still as God Created Me.

I am not a body. I am free. For I am still as God created me.

When it came time to choose residency training, eventually I settled on the field of pediatrics. I fell in love with children and their honest, direct presence with no hidden agendas. However, I felt great aversion toward working with dying children and dreaded being assigned to their cases. Yet our inner guide always has a plan for us; often the very thing we resist can be our greatest teacher.

One such child was Karen,[80] a seven-year-old girl with end-stage AIDS acquired from her birth mom, who was already dead. Karen lived with her father and her three-year-old brother, who were not infected by the virus. Karen's father admitted her to the hospital when he could not treat her persistent fevers at home. When she was diagnosed with AIDS, he stopped visiting. Yet Karen somehow understood and accepted this—sharing with a social worker that her father was afraid and that's why he stopped visiting.

Whenever I saw Karen on my morning rounds, she was often sitting up on her bed and vomiting into a basin, assisted by one of the hospital nurses or aides. She was on a dozen different medications. The nurses tried blending her medicines with applesauce or chocolate pudding, and even spacing them apart at different intervals. Karen's response was the same—yellow mustard vomit that blended with the hospital yellow mustard basin on her lap.

Karen suffered from an AIDS-related eye infection that caused her eyes to be highly sensitive to light. Her room was kept dark, with sunlight peeking softly through the blinds. Her large black eyes would find my gaze and stare unwaveringly at me. At seven years of age she was tiny, weighing 35 pounds—the average weight of a child half her age. Yet despite her small frame, I was aware of a wise presence about her.

"Dr. Seema, can you rub my tummy? *Please*, rub my tummy?"

I still needed to examine other children, yet I yielded to her imploring gaze. Slowly I began to rub her belly.

"How are you feeling now?"

"Better. Dr. Seema, can you stay a little? Look, we can color in my new coloring book."

Proudly she showed me the coloring book she had received from one of the hospital social workers. Karen especially loved coloring pictures of butterflies and flowers in bright, vivid hues. The nurses taped these on the walls near her bed. The cheerfulness of Karen's drawings contrasted sharply with the sterile white of the hospital walls, and the gaunt, lean profile of Karen's thin frame.

"Can you *please* read to me now? Just for a little while. *Please*."

Her gaze and her tone disarmed me. All the other tasks from my daily to-do list seemed to fade from my mind. Once more I acquiesced to her request. She pulled out *The Velveteen Rabbit*, a book we had read a dozen times. Soon her body relaxed against mine and she fell asleep. Perhaps for the first time in hours, she was pain-free.

For a moment, I forgot that Karen was a girl with AIDS who failed all our regimens and most likely would not live until her eighth birthday. I forgot my feelings of powerlessness and failure as her doctor who couldn't cure her, no matter how much I tried. Time stopped; just the moment was enough. No need to search or figure or plan. To rub tummies, to read, to color—to breathe and simply be was enough.

That night my sleep was restless. I dreamed of Karen and her huge eyes pleading with me. But for what? The Course teaches there are only two voices to be heard in our brothers and sisters: an expression of love or a call to love. Something within Karen reached my heart and filled me with an overwhelming sense of grief. I cried for hours. She helped me release grief that I too carried behind the exterior mask of the expert healer. The Course teaches that if we perceive suffering and pain, we carry this within our minds as well. Typically, as physicians or as healers, we focus our energies on fixing the patient outside. Yet we are the ones in need of healing as well.

The next morning, I decided that instead of just administering the details of medication management of children such as Karen, I would fully embrace this experience as a teacher to relieve suffering, both mine and that of the children. I felt inspired to let go of a senior project that was near completion. Instead, I began another project that was closer to my heart — a survey of about a hundred or so of my pediatric colleagues regarding their attitudes toward death and dying. Although I did not realize it at the time, I was taking my first step in opening to see the entire situation differently. As the Course teaches, a change in mind is the miracle that allows for deep, transformative healing that was ultimately the true yearning of my heart.

I soon discovered that most of my colleagues also felt challenged and often alone when coping with their own issues of grief and bereavement that arose as they cared for these children. Attending pediatricians who worked in fields with a higher mortality rate, such as hematology/oncology or intensive care, were more likely to view the death of a child as a personal failure. There was also no clear consensus among the pediatricians surveyed as to the degree of emotional involvement with a dying child and their family that was considered appropriate.

Other researchers have described how health care professionals caring for terminally ill patients experience two conflicting forces: the force of love and compassion "pressing toward involvement," and the force of fear that "presses towards avoidance and protection from painful feelings."[81] Once more, as the Course teaches again and again, we have only two choices: love or fear.

The nurses spent the most time with these children and knew them and their families on an intimate level. Yet I did not sense any aversion on their part to work with these children. This intrigued me. Following their example, I too began to spend more time with the children outside of my daily rounds. This provided a priceless opportunity to know them on a different level, just as children instead of patients with a terminal illness.

One African-American eight-year-old girl with AIDS spoke to me about how she perceived God—that He had not just one color but many colors, such as blue, orange, red and purple. As I read stories to these children or watched them play or draw, I came to realize that I did not know them at all. I could quote their medication regimens and their lab numbers, but they were still strangers to me. Somehow, I failed to see their core essence, which was pure, innocent, and whole—despite the external face of suffering.

The nursing staff routinely attended funerals of the children. As I accompanied them, I discovered an amazing opportunity to be with the family in their suffering and loss, instead of at a distance as the expert healer. Earlier, from a stance of fear and *separation*, I anticipated that attending funerals would trigger feelings of guilt and sadness at failing these children and their families. But in *joining* with the families, I was gifted with an overflowing showering of love and gratitude for my care. In listening to their families, I learned even more about these children and their lives outside the hospital—the birthday parties they attended, their rides on the local neighborhood fire truck, and their very first bike ride with training wheels around the block. My heart felt so much lighter. The Course teaches that "this world is full of miracles. They stand in shining silence next to every dream of pain and suffering, of sin and guilt." Once more, it was my perception that needed healing.

The pediatric department used the survey results to implement some educational resources to better assist the medical staff in coping with death and dying. With the help of some attending physicians, I modified Karen's medication regimen so she could spend her final days in an extended care facility where she could play, read, draw, and be loved and cared for like any other child. After her death, I received this note from her social worker:

> Karen passed away peacefully in her sleep last night. The week before was her eighth birthday. So, of

course, there was a big party :-) She even ate some cake and ice cream! She opened presents—books, markers, and crayons. She was very happy. We'll do a memorial service for her later in the week. Will send details.

The results of the survey were eventually accepted for publication in a national pediatric journal.[82] As I completed the final editing of the paper, I faced death on an even more personal level.

Thousands of miles away in a hospital room in New Delhi, India, my maternal uncle, Mamaji,[83] lay in a coma. My family and I were in constant touch with his family in India by phone and email. Despite the doctors' efforts, his condition steadily deteriorated.

One late afternoon, taking a break from my writing, I walked along one of the paved paths in Prospect Park in Park Slope, Brooklyn, where I lived and worked at the time. My feet instinctively turned toward the pond located at the center of the park. The tranquil waters shimmered with streaks of silver in the sunlight. I found my favorite tree and leaned against its sturdy trunk, allowing myself to release the deep fatigue of mind and body. I had been *doing* so much, between work, writing, and staying in contact with my relatives in India; there had been little time for *being* with my own feelings. The tree, the waters, and the sunlight slowly lulled me into a place of deep rest and relaxation. I closed my eyes and images of Mamaji floated through my mind from holidays spent in New Delhi.

I remembered Mamaji liked to wear white, freshly ironed, cotton *kurta-pajamas*[84], with crisp creases. His pockets were always full of chocolate and caramel toffees for his nieces and nephews. Mamaji took us to the local fairs where we enjoyed the different amusement park rides, the spicy Indian snacks dipped in aromatic chutneys, and the rich and creamy Indian sweets. As my childhood memories of Mamaji gently streamed through my mind, I felt increasingly mesmerized by the sunlight dancing on the shimmering waters of the pond.

And then I saw him.

Mamaji was smiling at me, dressed in his usual white cotton kurta pajama. But now he was bathed in an ethereal silver glow. He appeared robust and healthy, with red cheeks.

"Simmi, I'm fine. Don't worry about me. I'm completely fine."

He spoke to me in our native Punjabi with the intonation of his voice exactly as I remembered it from my childhood days. He also addressed me by my nickname, Simmi, as was his custom.

To the right of Mamaji stood my maternal grandmother, who had died more than a decade ago. She wore a traditional Punjabi style *salwar kameez*[85] with a scarf covering her head. It was the same outfit she wore in New Delhi when she cared for me while my mom was away at work. She stood there silently and seemed to be present only for Mamaji. Of her three sons, he was her favorite.

The grinding sound of plastic tires moving against the concrete path woke me from my reverie. A young child rode his Big Wheel tricycle while his mom followed behind on foot. She smiled at me as she passed by. I rubbed my eyes but Mamaji and my grandmother were nowhere to be found. Yet I could feel an unmistakable sense of peace, as if a huge burden had been lifted from my shoulders.

That same evening, my family received news that Mamaji had died. At first this surprised me. Based on my earlier vision, I expected Mamaji to heal and recover. My mom and her sister wept as they grieved the loss of their brother while I too shed tears as I mourned the loss of a special uncle. Yet amidst our sorrow, Mamaji's words echoed in my ears: *"Simmi, I'm fine. Don't worry about me. I'm completely fine."*

Slowly it dawned on me what I had just learned from Mamaji: *he was not just his body.* From thousands of miles away, transcending the barriers of life and death, across space and time, Mamaji connected with me when I was relaxed and open. If he were just a body limited to time and space, how would it be possible for us to connect? This meant that I, too, was more than just my body. And therefore, none of us is just a body that is born, lives briefly and ultimately dies! As Krishna taught Arjuna more than 2000 years ago in the *Bhagavad-Gita*, the body may be discarded just as we take off old clothes, but the indwelling spirit within us never ceases to be.[86]

My exploration of death and dying began with a simple desire to process and heal the loss and pain I experienced as I cared for my patients with terminal illness. Reading, research, writing the paper, spending time with the children and their caregivers, joining with my colleagues—all were steps that helped in healing. Yet an essential piece remained.

What is the purpose of all this suffering and loss?

Mamaji showed me that the only purpose is a radical forgiveness. This occurs when we are willing to bring all the events that our physical eyes and ears report—in this case, the suffering and ultimately, death of the body—to the inner teacher, so we may receive a healed perception, or a new way to understand *everything that seems to happen around us*. In his passing, Mamaji shared a priceless vision of healing, where there is no death and life continues, unhampered, unimpeded, unhindered, unconstrained, unburdened, and completely free.

I am not a body. I am free. For I am still as God created me.

I am not a body. I am free. For I am still as God created me.[87]

In the next chapter, we explore how setting our purpose of radical forgiveness right from the start when we encounter any challenge, can allow us to sink into a state of peace from where healing and miracles can flow.

CHAPTER 12

What Purpose Does This Experience Serve? What Is It For?

In any situation in which you are uncertain, the first thing to consider, very simply, is "What do I want to come of this? What is it for?" The clarification of the goal belongs at the beginning, for it is this which will determine the outcome.

In January 2004, Patti Fields, a student and teacher of *A Course in Miracles* discovered a lump in her breast. Initially, she was not very concerned because she had a history of benign breast cysts. Her doctor ordered a mammogram and then a sonogram which revealed there was a mass instead of fluid typical of a cyst. Now Patti was worried. A biopsy was performed the same day. About an hour later, she got a call from the doctor's office. The biopsy revealed aggressive cancer cells and her doctor was concerned because of her age as well as the nature of the cells. She was advised to return first thing the following morning for further testing.

At this point, Patti's worry turned to panic. She was in her mid-forties, a wife and mother of three young girls. Her mind began spinning in a million different directions. She began to have thoughts about what was going to happen. Images of needles sticking into the breast and the breast being removed floated through her mind.

However, she had also been a student of *A Course in Miracles* for the past few years. So, she did what she would normally do when faced with any problem: she turned to her circle of friends who were also Course students and began to apply what she was learning. Because of her background in ACIM, she was able to allow her mind to slow down and become quiet. And from this space of stillness, a more fundamental question emerged in her awareness:

What purpose does this experience serve?
What is it for?

As ACIM teaches, there are only two purposes in our mind:

(1) To experience love, peace and joy, which is our core essence; or:

(2) To experience fear, fragmentation and separation, which usually creates further distress and *dis*-ease.

We are encouraged by ACIM to decide our purpose or goal *beforehand*—not during the experience or afterward. This makes sense, just as it would be very practical to decide beforehand to go to the grocery store and not the bookstore if we want to pick up a gallon of milk. This is what I love about ACIM; it is immensely practical!

As Patti went deeper into a prayerful state, she became clear that she did have the choice to dedicate this experience of breast cancer to the healing of her mind so she could experience peace, joy and love. Yet to do this, she would need to let go of focusing on the body.

This is a radically different approach from the one that most of us apply when we encounter a health problem. Usually, many of us would be poring over the Internet trying to figure out a solution in the world of form. Perhaps we would weigh the benefits of conventional therapy against complementary/

alternative therapies. We might even label ourselves or others as neglectful or uninformed if we don't do our homework and educate ourselves as much as possible about our health condition and all the possible therapeutic options available. We believe that the more we know, the more likely we can resolve a problem.

The Course, however, teaches the opposite. We are asked to withdraw our attention from the many different aspects of a problem which tend to distract us and instead, go within. This does not mean that we don't engage with the world of medicine, let's say, if we are facing a health challenge. First, however, we go within to find stillness and guidance from our inner wisdom.

After Patti chose healing of her mind as the purpose of this experience of breast cancer and released her focus on the body, she became mindful of another deeper question: *This experience of breast cancer is going to be happening to the body — but is it happening to me?*

With this question came a huge shift in awareness. She describes this experience as one in which she felt lifted to an expanded state of awareness where there was just peace and love. The experience of breast cancer became a dream; it was like watching a movie. She realized she could do whatever was needed from a medical perspective, but her mind could rest in a state of love, tranquility, joy and absolute safety. This seemed to be the defining turn for her. An intense peace washed over her. The fear was gone. She fell asleep easily with a sense of excitement that she was about to have an experience of God.

For those readers who are new to ACIM, perhaps you may find it difficult to understand how Patti was able to be immersed in such peace after feeling so much fear, worry and even panic. Yet this is the beauty of the miracle. It is not something we do or make happen. Miracles are an experience of moving away from a state of fear to one of peace and love. We receive miracles to the capacity that we are willing and open to see our situation differently. Of course, we need great practice to do this, especially when we encounter a potentially life-altering diagnosis such as cancer.

When Patti went to the clinic the next day, she was in a heightened state of love and peace. All she perceived was love flowing from her and from everyone she met. She felt no concern for the body or what would happen. The nurses consoled her, expecting her to be fearful about the prognosis. Yet to Patti they were like angels singing. What they said about her pain, discomfort, or fear seemed silly as it was not her experience at all. When they touched her or when any procedure was done, she didn't feel any pain or discomfort. To the others it may have appeared that she was in shock, but Patti recalls feeling more aware, more present, and more connected to everyone around her.

She was taken to a private room and a doctor confirmed the findings of aggressive breast cancer. For Patti, from her expanded state of awareness, her body was a mere costume. When the doctor discussed the findings about the breast cancer, Patti felt as if the doctor were talking about a costume. She listened to what was being said, yet it didn't have any impact on her. She was not this costume, so it didn't occur to her to be fearful.

The doctor impressed upon Patti the gravity of her situation and urged her to call the surgeon the next day to proceed with further treatment. Perhaps the doctor felt Patti was in denial and not comprehending what she was telling her, so she kept repeating to her: "You need to do this first thing tomorrow morning. You'll do this, right? You'll call the surgeon tomorrow?"

Although Patti didn't share the doctor's urgency or fear, she didn't feel any resistance to doing what was asked of her. She felt no need to defend or explain anything. She simply reassured the doctor she would do as she had been instructed.

When she was with her family, Patti felt only love and peace. There was never any fear or concern about what would happen to her or them or what the outcome of all of this would be. However, she saw that her family was in fear and she determined to do her best to reassure them. She told them that all she was experiencing was love, that there was no fear, and she was completely safe. She asked them to watch and learn from her whenever they felt fear. Patti also kept her large extended family updated with daily emails. Later, many family members shared with her how her emails helped to comfort them and ease their fear.

The surgeon scheduled surgery right away but with a more conservative approach. She suggested a lumpectomy and lymph node resection followed later by a mastectomy instead of immediately doing a double mastectomy. Although other family members were uncomfortable with this approach, Patti didn't feel the need for a second opinion.

Following the surgery, Patti remained in a state of peace and love. There was no pain. There was no fear. There was only gratitude for everyone's help, for their making sure all her needs were met. While lying in bed after she returned home from surgery, Patti began to have thoughts of guilt. *I don't deserve all this care and concern. I'm not really struggling or experiencing any pain.*

Immediately she felt pain in her body. However, she quickly realized that the pain was directly related to her choice to listen to the unaware or sleeping mind, the monkey-mind that often feeds us thoughts about fear and guilt.

Later Patti explained, "Even though I was aware of the sudden change, I let the thoughts swirl around anyway. I went deep into experiencing the pain of not being worthy of love and the guilt for taking something I didn't deserve. I cried and cried. I remember thinking that the physical pain was my just desert. After a few hours, I decided that was enough of that. I literally said, 'I'm done listening to these thoughts.' I then started to repeat 'God' in my mind and my inner distress and physical pain went away."

Patti also remembered sitting in her friend's kitchen. Her friend, who cared for her wellbeing, provided Patti with information on all the dietary changes and supplements that could aid in the healing process and prevent the common side effects associated with chemotherapy or radiation—which seemed likely to be the next step. For a moment, Patti was overcome by fear, believing this cancer was indeed happening to her.

"It was as if I realized, 'Oh, you're talking about me!' The minute *me* was identified as the body, I became overwhelmed and afraid. After I left that meeting, I recognized that any time I left that right state of mind[88] and it seemed as if it was *me* they were talking about, I would sit quietly and repeat the word God. This would quickly return my mind back to peace."

About four days after her surgery, the surgeon called Patti and shared the pathology results. There was no cancer!

Patti's surgeon was at a loss to explain what had happened. She could not classify Patti's case according to any of her past experiences. Clearly, this was taking the surgeon outside of her accepted paradigm of healing. She even consulted with multiple labs for further testing. They all reported the same. There was not a single cancerous or even pre-cancerous cell to be found.

So, where did the cancer go?

To this day, Patti doesn't see the healing of the breast cancer as the real miracle. The Course defines miracle as an experience of love and freedom from fear. This healing of the mind *was* Patti's experience—being lifted to a state of awareness of the Self as having a dream of breast cancer and seeing clearly that what is happening within the dream does not change or harm us in any way. Patti shares that it was this awareness that kept her in a consistent state of peace and love, regardless of what the body experienced (aggressive breast cancer and surgery) or what others perceived (fear, danger, panic, or loss).

The Course teaches that all that is asked of us to experience miracles is our willingness to release what we think we know, so we may receive a healed perception of what is really happening. We cannot *think* or *visualize* or *talk* our way to this healed perception. From a place of deep surrender and letting go, when we are truly open to be taught that which is true and that which is false, we receive the miracle.

Patti's first step was her willingness to dedicate her experience to the healing of her mind. Next, she was willing to release her focus on the body. Finally, she could open to receive the answer from her inner wisdom. She was then given an inner spiritual vision without any filters, where all she perceived were love and safety—despite the external appearance of breast cancer.

Her family, friends, and doctors perceived from their filters of fear that she was in danger and she could die. However, Patti didn't experience this, nor did she judge their perceptions. There was no demand from anyone to be different in any way. There was no desire to fix, change, or heal anything. From this state of complete acceptance, Patti experienced a peace and love that was not of this world, and *the body's healing followed naturally.*

By setting our purpose firmly in mind before we move into any experience—whether it is a health problem or any other issue—we engage our inner resources and allow for healing that is richly rewarding and deeply transformative. As you read this chapter, if you are also facing a challenge in your life, ask yourself the same question that Patti asked when she first heard the word cancer:

What purpose does this experience serve?
What is it for?

Remember, do not let the circumstances decide your purpose but choose the purpose beforehand— that of peace, love and joy—and let this be the guiding light that leads your way. If you forget—and this can happen if the mind is not yet trained—you can simply stop and pause, and repeat this phrase to remind yourself:

What purpose does this experience serve?
What is it for?

When we choose to stay aligned with the purpose of experiencing consistent peace, love and joy, we cultivate miracle-mindedness—which I believe is the key to healing. In the following section, let us now explore what it means to be miracle-minded, and the tools that can help us. We also discuss the obstacles we may face along the way

PART THREE

What Is the Miracle?

CHAPTER 13

A Different Way to Understand Miracles

Miracles occur naturally as expressions of love. The real
miracle is the love that inspires them. In this sense everything
that comes from love is a miracle.

In the 1991 movie *The Doctor*, William Hurt portrays an aloof, arrogant, and self-absorbed surgeon who undergoes a radical transformation in his approach to patients because of his own diagnosis of cancer. In facing his own vulnerability and possible mortality, Hurt's character realizes that healing is much more than being skillful with a scalpel in the operating room.

Sometimes as physicians we need to become patients before we can practice healing that encompasses the heart along with the head. For me, my own illness radically shifted my practice of medicine and my overall approach to healing. The basic tool I offer is not any therapy, conventional or complementary, but rather a state of mind,[89] namely, *miracle-mindedness*[90] — in which we accept miracles as an ordinary part of life that can support us with whatever challenge we are facing.

I strongly believe miracle-mindedness is the key to healing. This state of mind is much deeper and broader than positive thinking.

Being miracle-minded means that although we understand we are worthy of miracles, we are never in charge of them. A gardener plants seeds and nurtures the soil with water, fertilizer, sunshine and love, yet she cannot force a flower to bloom. Likewise, we too cannot make miracles happen.

Positive thinking often presumes to know the best outcome in any given situation. Yet in miracle-mindedness, there is great humility. Often, we don't know the best possible outcome for our highest good or that of another. This leads to a state of being open, of being willing to learn and be taught by our inner teacher.

Sometimes, with positive thinking we feel like we are constantly going uphill. It seems to be a real chore to stay positive all the time. Yet in miracle-mindedness we have come to a place of trust and surrender so there is great peace. We understand that the miracle is not something to be chased outside us, to happen in some future point in time. Rather, the miracle is the state of peace, love and joy to be accepted within us right now, where we are, exactly as we are, warts and all.

Miracle-mindedness never denies the emotions that may come up along our path. We accept sadness, fear, anger, or any other upset we are feeling from moment-to-moment, day-to-day. Yet we are clear that we are always pointed true north: our guiding star is peace of mind and we want this above all else.

Positive thinking can be a step toward miracle-mindedness that brings us to inner peace. *A Course in Miracles* teaches that healing is the acceptance of inner peace. Peace is our rest. Peace is our strength. Peace offers us the ability to tune in to our inner wisdom, so we make choices that are in alignment with our highest good and the good of others.

The Merriam-Webster online dictionary defines miracle as "an extraordinary event manifesting divine intervention in human affairs."[91] The online Oxford Dictionaries define a miracle as a "welcome event that is not explicable by natural or scientific laws and is therefore attributed to a divine agency."[92]

Before I began to study the Course, miracles were something rare, like a miraculous healing from cancer, or winning the New York City lottery. After studying the Course, gradually I began to see that if we think of a miracle as a change of the external screen of our life and begin to focus on that, we lose the key to the Course and its profound message.

Miracles occur naturally as an expression of love. The real miracle is the love that inspires them. In this sense, everything that comes from love is a miracle.

If I were to summarize my experience of healing from chronic pain, I would express it this way. While on the outer plane I found myself negotiating an often confusing and disorienting maze of doctors, hospitals, surgeons, and medications, on the inner plane I was releasing fear and opening to love and inner peace.

I believe this deep inner shift was reflected in a healing of physical symptoms as well. Because my experience spanned several years, it is helpful to see that healing can be gradual; if it is not instantaneous, nothing is wrong. We are all opening to healing at the pace that works best for us. It seems that my mind was super-trained and vested in the world of medicine and the medical model, which is fear-based. I just needed more time to be ready and willing to release the fear and guilt and accept the miracle—which is simply a shift in perception from fear to love.

In the earlier chapters, we have explored examples of healing from seemingly serious medical diagnoses. Is the miracle then the healing of the body? And does healing from cancer constitute a big miracle yet healing from a cold is a small-scale miracle? That is what I first thought before I began to study the Course and even for some time after completing the workbook lessons. I was focused on *doing* and *becoming* and *having*, so even miracles were something to be achieved in the external world. And yes, to heal from cancer or a stroke did seem to be a more important miracle than any other. Yet as I went deeper I realized this was not true. Often, I didn't appreciate the many so-called smaller miracles that came my way.

There is no order of difficulty in miracles. One is not
"harder" or "bigger" than another. They are all the same.
All expressions of love are maximal.

For me, the Course is a process of exquisite surrender—a letting go into love with complete childlike trust and faith. It is not a manifesto of creating my reality but more of an invitation to accept my true reality and that of my brothers and sisters as the divine created us—complete, perfect, innocent, and wholly loving and lovable.

This seems very simple. "Let go and let God" is a phrase we often hear from well-meaning friends. Yet we all know how difficult it is to practice this even on good days and how almost impossible it is when we are experiencing pain or facing a chronic or life-threatening illness. That is why we all need miracles.

May the following chapters serve as a guide for you to also experience miracles. I hope you may learn from the many mistakes I made in my own healing process and yet understand that the mistakes were also part of the learning. Nothing was ever wrong, and I was doing the best I could with whatever my mind could accept at that point in time. Wherever you find yourself as you read this book is exactly where you are meant to be.

May you open to receive all the miracles you need along your path of healing!

CHAPTER 14

Physician, Heal Thyself: Opening to Miracles and the Process of Purification

The curriculum is highly individualized, and all aspects are under the Holy Spirit's particular care and guidance. Ask and He will answer.

In January of 2008, my life was hectic. While juggling a solo pediatric medical practice and single-parenting my then five-year-old son, I was also studying clinical homeopathy. Little did I realize a storm was brewing that would soon wipe away all the landmarks on my map of healing. None of my medical school training, my years of clinical practice, or even my study of complementary/alternative medicine could have prepared me for what happened next.

It all began with a pain in my tush. I still recall the exact moment when this pain began, during a heated argument with a close friend. Eventually our friendship dissolved, but the pain persisted. Doctors are often the worst patients! After a few weeks of self-treatment with diet and phone consults with my homeopath, reluctantly I paid a visit to my doctor. Thus began the work-up, involving visits to my gynecologist and then a gastrointestinal surgeon, who finally diagnosed a rectal abscess, which he drained. Soon afterward, the abscess developed into an anal fistula causing chronic pain.

The pain began each day after I stooled. During the day, it felt like a raging fire as the area filled with pus. I found that even standing, walking, and performing other simple movements were difficult. I would feel some relief when sitting or lying down and simply not moving. Then, I would brace myself in anticipation of the burning pain that took my breath away as I tried to stand up and move about. Finally, at some point during the day, the area drained, and the pain subsided somewhat to a smoldering ember. But it never went away, and in the morning the cycle began all over again.

My homeopath once asked about the drainage from the fistula site, particularly about any unusual odor. For those unfamiliar with homeopathy, such details can determine the homeopathic medication selection. I recall a master 20th century homeopath, who used the term *rotting carrion*—the decaying flesh of a dead animal—to describe the drainage from one of his patients' wounds. If I were to describe my experience with non-medical yet precise terminology, it would be *yuck!*

My mood ranged from constant irritation to full-blown rage. Despite the brave, smiling face I put on for my patients, cracks were showing through the *Miss Nice-Sweet-Kind-I-am-here-to-save-and-heal-the-world* persona. Unfortunately, my outbursts of anger occurred when I was in the company of my son and my parents, those with whom I felt most safe and loved. I felt I had an evil monster inside of me that I was doing my best to contain. Even at my workplace, my colleagues sensed something was wrong.

I felt too embarrassed to share my suffering. I felt a profound shame about all aspects of my illness: the location of the pain, the horrible, smelly drainage, and the fact that none of the trusted tools in my toolbox—including homeopathy and what I understood about mind-body medicine at that point—were helping. I felt like a complete failure.

126

The message was very clear:

Physician, heal thyself!

No longer could I care for others. I was now the patient. My parents flew in from New York City to help me care for myself and my son. Thus began my road of self-healing.

In addition to consulting with a gastrointestinal surgeon and remaining under the care of my primary care physician, I continued to pursue homeopathy. I also worked with a therapist skilled in mind-body medicine and I studied Louise Hay's books to understand which beliefs I needed to let go of and which new ones I needed to learn.[93] My homeopath and I tried over a dozen homeopathic medications. Initially, I would feel some relief but then the pain would return with a vengeance. I switched homeopaths and we tried a dozen more remedies. Once again, the results were the same.

I was determined to heal the natural way and was adamant about not doing anything invasive. I would not even take over the counter pain medications, such as Tylenol or Advil. I was convinced there was a higher purpose to this suffering. Even if I had to tolerate severe pain, that's what I was going to do, dammit! So, I practiced affirmations. I did breathing exercises. I practiced yoga postures that focused on the lower chakra centers. I modified my diet. I drew pictures that showed healing of the fistula. I visualized. I chanted different prayers. I even tried to practice forgiveness, but instead, I ended up uncovering a litany of more grievances with the outside world. These included my parents, my upbringing and the Indian culture, my failed marriage and the ensuing divorce, my friend who I felt had betrayed me, my body, the surgeon, my homeopath, etcetera, etcetera, etcetera. Obviously, I needed help in my forgiveness practice!

No matter what I tried, the pain was relentless. Finally, I conceded defeat and underwent a minor surgery in the summer of 2008, about six months after the beginning of this ordeal. I felt some relief and was hopeful that now my life would finally return to normal. To some extent this was the case. The pain continued but at a lower level and I could care for myself and my son again. However, whenever I encountered a stressful situation, the pain escalated. I used a combination of rest, homeopathy, and other self-care methods. I didn't return to the surgeon to explore other options. In my mind, the surgery was still something bad, representing failure because it wasn't natural healing.

In retrospect, when I reflect on this challenging time, I feel a deep wave of compassion for myself. That I continued to function and care for myself and my son, despite the varying degrees of pain I was experiencing, *was* a miracle. My experience taught me that we really cannot judge the events in our lives. What may be perceived as a failure may offer a rich opportunity for deep transformative healing. According to *A Course in Miracles*, we cannot put ourselves in charge of healing ourselves, for we cannot tell *advance* apart from *retreat*. We judge as failures some of our greatest advances, while we evaluate as success some of our deepest retreats.

The pain ultimately served as a catalyst for clarifying what was of value in my life and releasing what no longer was helpful. During those months as I lived with chronic pain, I reflected on a profound question that a Buddhist teacher asked the audience during a death and dying conference I attended in NYC:

If you knew you just had one year to live,
what would you do differently?

The answer became crystal clear: I was ready to release my pediatric medical practice. I realized it was serving my patients and their families but no longer nurturing me. What was once my joy now felt like burden. Over the course of a few months, I said goodbye to the clinical practice of pediatric Western medicine. With the blessings and support of my parents, without whom I could not have made such a huge decision, I set up my own practice in holistic medicine. Previously I treated only children and adolescents but now I felt comfortable working with adults as well, acting as a consultant in homeopathy, yoga, and mind-body medicine.

For the next five years, in addition to building my holistic practice, I taught many seminars in mind-body medicine, homeopathy, yoga and meditation, both in the community and nationally, as well as at the local medical school in Rochester. I met new teachers and colleagues in the field of mind-body medicine and found a new homeopathy mentor who prescribed homeopathic medications that were helpful whenever my fistula pain acted up.

Despite the fistula pain still present in my life with varying intensity, I felt an immense sense of freedom. Finally, I could practice medicine the way I wanted by spending as much time with each client as needed to be fully present to their story. Many clients deeply appreciated my work. I could also rest, care for myself and my son, and still have time to read, research, and study. From today's vantage point, I see how the pain ultimately served as a bridge to support my unwinding from the traditional MD role, step-by-step. First, I was given the pediatric practice with integrative focus. Then came the practice of holistic medicine with focus on mind-body medicine (along with homeopathy, yoga, and

Ayurveda). Eventually, this led to my current work in Coaching for Inner Peace.

Yet the first two were stepping stones or assignments— essential parts of a larger curriculum designed especially for me by my inner teacher. Without these intermediate steps, I couldn't have written this book. As ACIM teaches, for everyone, "the curriculum is highly individualized, and all aspects are under the Holy Spirit's[94] particular care and guidance."

Gradually my pain disappeared, and I thought I was healed. However, in my holistic practice, I encountered many clients with chronic pain whom I was unable to help. This frustrated me. I recall sitting up many nights poring over homeopathy texts to solve difficult cases from my practice.

By this stage in my career, I understood the role that diet, exercise, medications—conventional and alternative, such as homeopathy or herbs—played in healing. I thought I understood the power of the mind through my study of mind-body medicine.

Yet I felt I was holding many threads but not seeing how they could weave together into a beautiful tapestry. All the elements of healing lay before me—but how did they all fit into a cohesive, unified whole? Moreover, how could this new approach serve those who seemed to be still suffering with chronic pain or other chronic conditions? How could I help them be free from pain? I felt an inner nudge that whispered, *"There must be another way. There must be another way."*

In the spring of 2012, this other way showed up in my life as *A Course in Miracles* and Patti Fields, whom you met in Chapter 12. Patti became my first ACIM mentor, connecting me to a much larger community of ACIM teachers and students. Right from the beginning, I felt an inner sense that if I stayed with this course of study, all my questions about healing—past, present and future—would be answered.

So I dove in deep. I attended every workshop Patti offered. I spent countless hours poring over the ACIM book and watched hundreds of videos of teachers of ACIM on *YouTube*. Eventually, I enrolled and subsequently completed the two-year online training in ACIM through David Hoffmeister and Living Miracles Monastery.

I was fascinated by the idea of miracles. Learning that miracles could be part of healing felt like the missing piece that had eluded me ever since I first set foot in medical school. By finding ACIM, a manual that could teach me about the principles of miracles, I felt like I had won the million-dollar jackpot. The same devotion I had for homeopathy was now channeled into a deep exploration of ACIM.

Miracles are everyone's right, but purification is necessary first.

The idea that miracles are everyone's right felt so liberating. Why should anyone be denied a miracle? Yet why did we need this purification process? Why couldn't we all just receive miracles of healing? What is this purification process, anyway? Over time, I realized that purification refers to the radical decluttering that appears to be what most of us need in our lives. This is not just about releasing physical objects (which of course is helpful) but also a deeper letting go of all those ideas, beliefs, concepts, and interpretations that are derivatives of fear-based thinking. As David Hoffmeister shares, what most of us usually need is a washing away of those misperceptions that block us from experiencing a steady flow of love and peace in our daily lives. According to

David, forgiveness is essentially an ongoing and continuous process where the mind is rinsed over and over, much like washing clothes in the laundry. Wash, rinse, repeat. Wash, rinse, repeat.

Often, we cling to our ideas and beliefs *even when they create pain for us.* I like to share the following Buddhist tale with my clients, about three different types of horses. The first type is very easy to train and just needs a nod or glance from the trainer to follow orders. The second type needs more work, perhaps a pull from the reins or more effort on the part of the trainer to get the horse to do whatever is required. The third type of horse is so obstinate and headstrong, he needs a good beating before he will follow orders.

We prefer to think that we're like the first horse, but really, we're like the third one. Usually, we need adversity— whether it is an experience of chronic pain, the loss of a relationship or job, or some other painful experience—to serve as the necessary catalyst for true change. It is during times like these, when things seem to be falling apart and life as we knew it seems to be slipping away despite all our efforts to keep it together, that we are ripe to release our old ways of inhabiting our lives. We are ready to reach for the other way—the way of love and peace, rather than fear and clinging.

Soon this would be my experience as well. As I fell deeper and deeper in love with ACIM, the outer landmarks of my life changed in unexpected ways. My clients began to dwindle, so again I had to accept a regular medical job to support myself and my son. A close friendship unraveled despite my sincere efforts to cement and salvage it. I felt I was in freefall; nothing made sense anymore.

Yet the one thing that remained constant and continued to prosper was my relationship to ACIM and the community of teachers and students connected to ACIM. This was my life preserver, the raft that was keeping me afloat in a vast ocean of uncertainty. It provided my only palpable connection to life and safety.

In this time of deep transition, the pain from the fistula returned with even greater force than before. Little did I know that the next several months would bring many miracles in my life—but not before the necessary process of purification.

CHAPTER 15

Going Deeper with Mind Watching and Mind Training: What Is this Pain All About?

You must look upon your illusions and not keep them hidden, because they do not rest on their own foundation.... For beneath them, and concealed as long as they are hidden, is the loving mind that thought it made them in anger. And the pain in this mind is so apparent, when it is uncovered, that its need of healing cannot be denied.

Earlier in my training in homeopathy, I learned about *obstacles to cure*.[95] When treating my clients, I tried to not only prescribe the correct homeopathic remedy but also explore the lifestyle factors that could block healing. This included poor diet, lack of exercise, or other challenges in the mental, emotional and social realm that needed to be addressed to facilitate healing.

Similarly, when we negotiate the inner journey of the mind while facing a chronic emotional and/or physical challenge, including chronic pain, we meet many obstacles along the way. Drawing from my personal as well as professional experience, I want to share roadblocks that often arise along our path to healing.

Although this chapter will address errors that come up in the context of ACIM practice, I believe this information can be helpful even if you're not practicing ACIM.

Obstacle #1: Denial – "it's not real" or "everything is an illusion"

When the pain returned, I simply ignored it. ACIM teaches that "true denial is a powerful protective device" that allows us to stay in the aware or awake mind. We look beyond appearances and ask our inner wisdom to help us see our situation differently, that is, through the lens of love and light instead of fear and lack. Yet in my case, my denial came from my sleeping or unaware mind.

The fistula felt as if I were sitting atop something that weighed me down and was uncomfortable, yet I wanted to pretend it wasn't there. Even when practicing positive thinking, we can still be holding onto a whole boatload of hidden subconscious beliefs about lack and limitation. The positive affirmations are like icing on a cake of mud—certainly not very appetizing let alone healing.

David Hoffmeister and his students refer to this as *metaphysical ghosting*.[96] We feel fearful, angry, and depressed, yet we say, "Everything is fine." We hide our pain by reciting ACIM concepts such as "All of this is an illusion anyway" or "The body is not real so there is really no problem." We seem to be applying the ACIM metaphysics yet the words we use are incongruent with our state of mind. I consider this a form of *pseudo peace*—a deceptively calm state beneath which brews a volcano of emotions.

Obstacle #2: Getting lost in the chatter of the monkey-mind

Within a day or so of being in denial, I was limping and barely able to move. Finally, when the pain reached a crescendo, I surrendered to what the pain asked of me—to simply stop and listen. But all I heard was a swirling storm of discordant and disturbing thoughts that were spinning my head in a thousand directions, each demanding my attention.

What had I done wrong? Was it my diet? Was it the stress from my job? Was I holding a grievance? Should I not have taken this job — was I supposed to be doing something else? Maybe I needed to quit the job. Was it something I was thinking? What was wrong? What had I done wrong, and if so, what could I do to fix it?

As a pediatric intern, I wondered how my supervising senior pediatricians could hear the heartbeat or lung sounds of a crying infant. With all that crying and sometimes even screaming, how did they *really* ascertain a heart murmur or wheezing? I soon realized they didn't possess any magical or mystical powers. Rather, they had practiced over the years with hundreds, perhaps thousands, of crying infants and toddlers. By the end of my internship, I had also gained some proficiency. Whenever I examined a crying baby, I learned to focus *only* on the heart or lung sounds. It didn't matter if my patients were crying or screaming (as many were!) in a noisy pediatric intensive care unit or busy emergency room.

Similarly, through a solid practice of ACIM or, for that matter, any meditation or self-reflection practice, we learn to accept the chatter or even screaming of the monkey-mind, but it is no longer our master. We know that the answers we need to negotiate our path to healing are found in the stillness beneath the clamor of the monkey-mind. We learn to wait until we discern that still small voice and let it guide our path.

Obstacle #3: Seeing the present through the lens of past experience

When the pain returned, I felt engulfed by a mushrooming cloud of terror. Images of my experience of the fistula flashed across my mind. I braced myself for a round of needles, surgeons, drainage, blood tests, and more pain. In a state of panic, my mind reverted to the past.

My mind is preoccupied with past thoughts.

We know from the field of neuroplasticity that our daily thought patterns create neurochemical pathways or grooves in our brains and usually we tend to fall into thinking along these pre-existing tracks.[97] That's why changing our minds feels so arduous. Yet each time we make a new decision about seeing things differently, we create a new mental groove or pathway. I refer to these as *baby pathways*, just like seeds in a garden. For these baby pathways to become an established part of our neural wiring, they need our consistent attention and practice. Just as we nurture seeds with water and sunshine, so we need to cultivate the garden of our mind with a steady, devoted practice. Only then can we free ourselves from our habitual thought patterns and become open to receive miracles.

Obstacle #4: Doing a spiritual bypass

Although I was now ready to face my pain and not get lost in the surface chatter of the monkey-mind or revert to the past, I was still not done. There was more work to do! I found it very difficult to simply not want a solution that would take the pain away. Why couldn't I just receive a miracle of healing? Why did I have to go through this painful experience *all over again?*

I didn't realize that I was seeking a *spiritual bypass*—a term coined in the 1980s by psychologist John Welwood. He defines a spiritual bypass as a way "to use spiritual ideas and practices to sidestep or avoid facing unresolved emotional issues, psychological wounds, and unfinished developmental tasks." We try "to rise above the raw and messy side of our humanness before we have fully faced and made peace with it."⁹⁸ With a spiritual bypass, we reach for our spiritual practice not as a support in healing *through* a situation, but rather as a ploy for *bypassing* the situation and avoiding it altogether.

A spiritual bypass is just an attempt to help us feel better. My desire to receive a miracle was certainly understandable. Who wants to be in pain? Yet while I wanted the miracle to change my *outward* experience (healing of the fistula and my pain), I was unwilling to look at the healing that needed to occur *inwardly*. I wanted the miracle but was unwilling to look at the stuff beneath the pain. I simply wanted to bypass this essential step of going within and looking at my mind—which is the core teaching of ACIM, and part-and-parcel of any spiritual self-inquiry practice.

Using tools of self-reflection, journaling, long walks in nature, and many heart-to-heart conversations with other ACIM students and teachers, I began to see how the fistula was a perfect symbol of self-judgment and guilt still being held inside my mind. The fistula was smelly, painful, and utterly disgusting. The feeling of aversion was so strong, if it were possible, I would have crawled out of my body. It felt like a deep self-loathing—a sense of feeling so tainted, no amount of rinsing could wash this away. So, I reached for the miracle instead of facing these uncomfortable feelings. And then I felt angry that God wasn't listening to me!

Over time, it became clear that the fistula was a symbol not only of guilt and self-loathing, but also of crucifixion, martyrdom and sacrifice. When I was in pain, it gave me permission to blame others for my problems, to feel sorry for myself. I was playing the role of a martyr—being crucified by others and forced to sacrifice myself at their expense. *Poor Seema, bad world, look how much I'm suffering!*

I was amazed that I didn't see this before—and this is the miracle: *a new way to relate to our experience through the lens of nonjudgmental awareness and acceptance rather than self-condemnation or judgment of others.* I learned to lean gently into the pain and not push it away. I realized it was here to teach me something and there was no reason to resist, hide, or run away. This was not easy to do, but with practice it became less difficult.

Obstacle #5: Making decisions by ourselves instead of becoming still and asking for guidance

When we face a challenging health situation, often we confront difficult decisions. Do we take this medication, or not? Do we say yes to chemotherapy and/or radiation, or not? Do we need to consult with another doctor, or perhaps an alternative practitioner, or not? Do we say yes to surgery, or not? The list of questions and decisions can seem endless, leaving us feeling heavy, confused and maybe even panicked.

Many clients I work with feel overwhelmed not just by their emotional and/or physical pain, but also by the bewildering medical and mental health maze that lies before them. Unfortunately, in today's health care system, this seems to be typical of any situation that is chronic in nature. This confusion is precisely the opposite of the miracle-mind, which lives in a space of ease and flow, like a gentle breeze flowing through the windows on a summer evening. Yet we can't feel this breeze if our windows are shut. When we allow the monkey-mind to guide us instead of listening for the still small voice within our hearts, we lock the windows of our miracle-mind. We separate ourselves from our rich treasure of inner wisdom.

In my case, the need to find a way to enter a space of stillness on a consistent basis became essential to my healing. Without it, I felt as if I were driving my car in a winter storm with the front window covered with snow. Meeting with an accident was not only probable but inevitable. Fortunately, with a deepening practice of ACIM, I found myself able to move through the superficial layer of noise and static and reach that place of stillness where I received the answers to guide me. Although I realized my mind needed training and willingness to discern the voice of the inner guide, I knew it could be done.

The prayer I often used whenever I faced one of those key decision points was very practical: *What am I to do? What would be most helpful right now?*

I didn't realize it then, but these words are an abbreviated version of a prayer included in Lesson 71 where we are asked to pray to God to reveal His plan to us by asking Him very specifically:

What would You have me do?
Where would You have me go?
What would You have me say, and to whom?

For many of you reading this, perhaps the words God, His or Him don't feel comfortable. Please feel free to substitute words such as love or peace or the universe. When I'm working with children or young adults, I explain to them that we have two parts of our mind. One is like the cartoon monkey Curious George—mischievous, always on the move, never able to still itself. The other part is the *Yoda-mind* (Yoda refers to the well-known character from the *Star Wars* film)—

the wise, stable, steady part that contains all the answers we need for any problem we may face. Although Curious George can be playful, when we face a serious situation, which part of the mind would you choose for leading you out of your trouble? My young friends unanimously choose Yoda as their guide.

In my case, by listening deeply for that still small voice, I was guided to continue to work with my surgeon and take medications for pain as needed. I also used tools of self-care, such as rest, meditation, journaling, self-reflection, and walks in nature. Added to these practices were many heart-to-heart conversations with other ACIM students and teachers. Although there is no formula for healing, letting our inner guide direct our path certainly seems to be a good place to start.

Obstacle #6: Choosing separation over joining

When we are sick with a cold or headache, often we separate ourselves to rest and recuperate. Eventually we recover and reconnect with others. Often, however, when we are experiencing chronic pain, either physical or emotional, we may live in a state of chronic isolation. This may or may not be apparent to us at the physical level. We may be surrounded by family and friends, yet we are not feeling connected to them.

In my experience with chronic pain, sometimes I did need to be alone so I could rest and heal. However, on other occasions, I was aware that I used the pain to isolate myself from others. Even when I chose to separate myself, deep inside my heart I longed for connection and companionship. However, I did not feel safe to expose and look at previous hurts and losses associated with past experiences with friends and family members, so they could be healed. Instead, I found it easier to use pain as a good excuse to limit my contact with others. I soon discovered that many people suffering from chronic pain feel conflicted between a desire for intimacy and social connection and a fear of joining with others. Instead of reaching out to connect, they end up choosing isolation and separation.

This choice for separation can occur even when surrounded by friends and family. Many of my clients who face chronic pain feel they cannot share what is truly in their hearts with those they love the most. They are afraid of being ridiculed or shamed. They may also feel that no one else will understand the pain they face daily. Social media may allow for joining but often it cannot substitute for the old-fashioned way of simply speaking one's heart while sharing a meal with a trusted friend or family member.

Dean Ornish, a physician and researcher best known for his groundbreaking studies demonstrating how comprehensive lifestyle changes can reverse even severe coronary heart disease without resorting to drugs and surgery, states:

> There isn't any other factor in medicine—not diet, not smoking, not exercise, not stress, not genetics, not drugs, not surgery—that has a greater impact on our quality of life, incidence of illness and premature death from all causes than loneliness and isolation.[99]

A phrase from ACIM sums this up beautifully:

> *Healing is the effect of minds that join, as sickness comes from minds that separate.*

In my case, after feeling supported with my new knowledge about separation and isolation, I did whatever was necessary to care for myself, which included rest, naps and medication. However, I also made a conscious decision to join with others as best as I could *even* when I had pain. I was determined not to let my ego mind use my pain to separate and isolate me from others, but rather, *to give pain the purpose of joining and connection.* I made sure not to do this from a sense of obligation or any sort of external pressure to please others, or from any sense of false bravado about how I wasn't going to let the pain knock me down. Instead, I connected first with my Yoda-mind and let its wisdom guide my outer connection with friends and family. Ultimately, ACIM practice is not about what bodies are doing or not doing but about the healing of the mind. In joining with others physically, I made a clear decision to turn *away* from the ego's use of the body for separation and isolation and move *toward* the inner guide's use for joining and connection. I recall how each time I made this choice, I felt better emotionally as well as physically.

From my current vantage point, when I recall this time, I can feel a sense of being completely inward-focused. Although the pain fluctuated, it was no longer the center of my attention. Rather, with the help of the inner guide and many mighty companions, I was steady in shining light inside my mind.

Only one key step still remained: that of surrender and releasing the error of level confusion. We explore this deeply in the next chapter.

CHAPTER 16

Arriving at the Miracle: Above All Else, I Want Peace

Miracles transcend the body. They are sudden shifts into invisibility, away from the bodily level. That is why they heal.

In my traditional as well as my holistic practice, whenever I worked with clients facing a chronic challenge such as physical pain, I focused on elucidating factors surrounding their pain. When did the pain tend to occur? How would they describe it? Which factors seemed to make it better? Which made it worse? In this way, the client and I *together* became expert about their pain and devised strategies to manage it.

In my own experience with pain, I also became an expert. With support from my homeopathic doctor as well as my surgeon, I learned to manage the pain so I could function. This was certainly a helpful stage along the road toward greater self-awareness as it related to the pain experience. However, for permanent healing, a radical step remained: *I had to let go of my focus on the pain (and ultimately the body) altogether.* ACIM refers to this obstacle as *level confusion.* I needed to move through this confusion before I could experience a permanent healing of the pain.

What is Level Confusion?

When we face a chronic health care challenge, often we feel that by knowing as much as possible about our problem and researching all the treatment options, we are most likely to succeed in reaching a successful resolution. We become very busy *doing* and often don't spend time *being*. We are habituated to believe that to heal we need to fix something at the level of the body. If we have pain in the knee, then we need to fix the knee. If we have depression or anxiety, we need medication to fix the chemicals in our brain. ACIM states that this is level confusion, defined as "the belief that what is amiss on one level can adversely affect another." According to ACIM, the body, which includes the brain, is merely an effect of the mind; only the mind is causative. As we discussed in chapter 4, the body does not even have the solidity that we perceive because it is mostly empty space.

We *confuse levels* if we ascribe causation to the physical when it lies at the level of the mind only. We then feel personally responsible for fixing whatever is wrong at the level of the body. However, ACIM teaches that the body is merely an instrument that follows what the mind decides or interprets. We can think of the body as a thermometer that reflects the ambient room temperature. The thermometer does not cause the heat or the cold. So, the problem is not with the body but at the level of the mind; specifically, the way that the mind perceives the body and how the body is being used. *All illness is really mental illness.*

Cause and Effect: Going from Inside to Outside

For those of you reading this who are new to ACIM or perhaps have a medical or nursing background, this may feel too out there. How can a sports injury, which seems to be caused by a hit to the head by a soccer ball, or skin cancer, which appears to be related to excess exposure to the sun's ultraviolet rays, be a mental illness?

As someone with more than 30 years of experience in traditional as well as complementary/alternative medicine, I can tell you that once I really understood what ACIM was teaching, I felt a profound sense of relief. Finally, I could devote my attention 100% to working on exposing and uprooting the *cause* of illness which lay in the mind. I no longer had to spend time tinkering with the *effects* that were reflected in the body. Let me illustrate with another example.

Imagine that we rent a theater for a private screening. The person in the projector room starts the movie but after watching it for a few minutes, we realize we don't want to see the rest of it. We would prefer to watch a different movie. The most practical and effective way to change what's playing on the theater screen would be to ask the person in the projector room to change the film in the projector. It would be silly to stand in front of the screen and try to change the movie from the *outside*. Rather, we need to change it from the *inside*, or at the source of its projection.

Similarly, when facing a chronic illness, we need to change the script that is running the show from the *inside* and not just attempt to fix the body from the *outside*. ACIM invites us to exert control over our minds, *where we have the power and responsibility to do so*. Often, we don't have control over our behavior or our bodies.

Let's consider another example that illustrates this concept more concretely. Think about friends and family members in your social circle who struggle with addiction, perhaps to cigarettes, alcohol, or other substances. Even if they know these substances are harmful to their bodies, often they are unable to change their behavior. Many facing addictions find it is helpful to work with Alcoholics Anonymous or other 12-

step programs that focus on releasing the inner beliefs that give rise to addictive behavior.

With a deepening practice of ACIM, we work with our inner wisdom to train our minds to access deeper and more consistent states of peace. Health is essentially the byproduct of a peaceful mind. Mental as well as physical health *is* inner peace.

A Combination of Magic and Miracle

This doesn't mean that we say the body isn't real, which would be an example of metaphysical ghosting as discussed in the previous chapter. Or that it is wrong to seek help from a doctor, work with a therapist, or take medications. In fact, ACIM says we may have so much fear when facing a challenging situation, we need to use these outside agents to lower our fear level so our mind can slowly open to the miracle. ACIM refers to this as using a combination of *magic* and the miracle to heal. The miracle reflects the mind opening to its own inherent power and ability to create. Magic, in the context of ACIM, ascribes power to outside agents such as medications to produce a change in our bodies, instead of acknowledging that it is really the mind that is causative. Both sickness and healing are decisions made first in the mind.

Once again, if you are new to ACIM or if you have a nursing or medical background, here is where you may feel resistance. I also struggled with these ideas. Deep down I realized that I was on the verge of a major paradigm shift that would crumble the medical model of health and illness that I'd spent so many years learning to master.

Let's look at this another way. Imagine you dream that you become ill. In the dream you seek help from a doctor who prescribes medications to help you recover. Of course, while you are dreaming, you believe your illness is real, the doctor is real, and the medications have real therapeutic effects. But when you awaken, even though the dream felt real, you know it was just a dream. There was no illness, no doctor, and the medications were not real either. We can say that the medication in the dream had a sort of magical property, an effect that in the context of the dream seemed to heal. Yet this is not reality. The true healing came when awakening from the dream—when you realized you were never ill to begin with. It was all a dream. In the context of healing, the miracle—a shift in perception from fear to love—is an awakening from a dream of seeing yourself at the mercy of an illness or some external situation (a state of fear) to the realization of your innate power to choose and align with love.

Level Confusion and the Placebo Effect: The Future of Medicine

At first glance, these ideas from ACIM seem far-fetched and impossible to believe. However, let's consider the placebo studies we reviewed in chapter 2. These studies pointed out that healing and recovery from illness are not so much about which therapy is used as about the meaning and interpretation that the patient assigns to this therapy. In my 30-plus years in the medical field, I have found this to be true.

The common denominator of healing lies not in diet, medications, surgery, or even exercise. Any or all of such therapies can be helpful, meaning different people will benefit from different therapies. The key factor to healing seems to be the *attitude* of the person using the therapy. The placebo research supports this conclusion.

By transcending the obstacle of level confusion and by taking power away from any one therapy, we place it where it belongs—in the mind of the patient who is about to receive it. This therapy may be alternative or traditional; it could be a medicine or a placebo. It could even be surgery.

Neuroscience and neuroplasticity research have already revealed significant evidence of the power of the mind. These findings will continue to grow. The fields of healing and medicine will evolve into ways to help patients transform their outlook, perception, and interpretation *before* they even receive medications or treatments. I feel fortunate to be a part of this exciting evolutionary process in medicine.

Practical Application: Using a Combination of Magic and the Miracle

In my case, although I was aware of ACIM's teachings, I knew I still needed time to go within and allow the inner healing. I also knew that I couldn't really focus and go within when I felt pain. Both sitting and resting helped to alleviate the pain. I didn't seem to do well with pain medications containing codeine, so I avoided these, but I did use medications such as Tylenol or Advil, or at times, homeopathic medications. After taking these measures, I then would read a passage from ACIM or listen to a video from an ACIM teacher, and reflect. Or I would just journal or go within to see what was going on inside my mind, spending time praying and meditating as guided. At times, I would join with another mighty companion who held a safe space for me to expose thoughts of guilt, fear, sadness, unworthiness, or whatever seemed to be coming up. Movies also inspired me; they helped me to see myself and my experience in a different way.

Within my mind and heart, I felt a deep willingness to pursue this process of inner healing for as long as necessary. By this time, after having lived with the pain for so many years and having tried many therapies, including surgery, I was convinced that the cause of my pain was not in the body. No matter what I tried on the physical level, the pain persisted. With my background in mind-body medicine and with an intensive study of ACIM, I arrived at an undeniable clarity that a deeper root in the mind needed healing. This clarity and conviction were the undoing of level confusion for me. Finally, I was able to place the cause of my illness where it belonged—in the mind. At the same time, I used magic or external agents, such as medication, surgery, and homeopathy when and how I felt guided to do so.

Using Levels of Mind

I realized that the more I tried to put my attention on the pain in the body instead of pulling back and really looking at what was going on in my mind, the more I struggled. It was like trying to focus on the leaf of a tree and the whole tree at the same time. Also, the more I focused on getting rid of the pain, the more it persisted.

I found myself often using David Hoffmeister's Level of Mind[100,101,102] process. This helped me to turn my attention away from the pain and instead, to step back to see what was going on within my mind. I learned to look beneath the pain to expose all the false beliefs. Each time I went through this process and emptied the mind of still more false beliefs, I felt more open and less fearful.

Being With the Pain, Watching the Mind

I would also let myself simply *sit* with the pain. I would watch the stream of thoughts pass by like clouds in the sky— thoughts and beliefs in self-judgment, sacrifice, guilt, punishment, unworthiness, helplessness and even self-hatred. I allowed the emotions of sadness, anger, fear and frustration to flush up. Although these painful beliefs and emotions were difficult to face, this time I didn't fall into the ego trap of thinking I was to figure anything out. Or that I was wrong or guilty, or not practicing the Course correctly. Or that I had done something wrong and that's why I was being punished with pain. I just simply sat with whatever came up.

The Decision for Peace

Eventually, it became clear to me that the healing must be experienced in this moment. It did not exist anywhere else. There was no purpose in going into the past or the future to figure out the answer to my pain. I needed to feel the relief and answer right now, right here.

So, I found myself simply becoming an observer of what was happening in my mind. I watched as my mind went to the body and the pain and told me a story about it. Each time I would *pull back*. Once again, I became the observer, the watcher. I was determined not to be distracted by the body anymore. I couldn't control what my body was feeling in the moment, but I was willing to claim the power of my mind to choose and experience peace.

This was my turning point. I desired peace of mind *above all else*. The prayer of my heart was simple. I wanted peace—no matter what my body was experiencing. I was tired of fighting myself, the pain, and the world of doctors, surgeons, and treatments. I was tired of trying to figure this out. I took off my doctor's hat and even stopped trying to be a good ACIM student. I simply had no energy to fix or change anything. I just wanted to be at peace—even if there was pain.

Arriving at the Miracle

I recall waking up one morning with a sense of anticipation that I had somehow broken through some deeply held beliefs surrounding illness, pain, the body, sickness, medicine, and healing. I felt inspired to get up earlier than usual, so I could sit in quiet before becoming busy with my son and the chores of the day. Since I still felt some pain, I did whatever I felt I needed so I could sit comfortably. I also took pain medications that seemed to help.

As I deeply surrendered to the moment, I slowly came to realize I was experiencing pain, *yet I was not this pain.* I could feel a distinct presence within me that was completely pain free and was simply watching this experience of pain. Between this presence and the experience of pain was simply love. I was not to push the pain away or try to fix it. I was to just allow myself and this pain to receive love. *The pain had been a call for love all along.* Caring for myself through whatever means— rest, food, medicine, surgery, and so forth—were merely different forms to answer that call. I heard the inner guide saying to me gently:

> *There is nothing else to do.*
> *Nowhere else to go.*
> *Nothing to make happen.*
> *Just be here. Just be here right now, right here.*
> *Just receive this love.*
> *Just allow yourself to be bathed in love.*

Somehow, I arrived at a moment when all sense of blame, shame, guilt, and judgment fell away. I felt an incredible sense of peace and love flood through me. In retrospect, I came to what ACIM calls a *holy instant*:

In the holy instant it is understood that the past is gone...
*The stillness and the peace of **now** enfold you in perfect*
gentleness. Everything is gone except the truth.

If I could describe it now, it felt like I had been led by my inner wisdom on an inward journey to the center of my mind:[103]

THE LAYERS OF MIND THAT FORM PERCEPTION

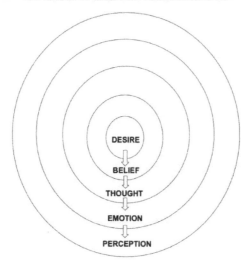

- Below the level of perception (an experience of a body feeling physical pain)

- Below the realm of emotions (fear and frustration about the pain and why it was not getting better)

- Below the realm of thoughts about the pain (what I needed to do, what would happen, what had caused this pain)

- Below the realm of beliefs held in the mind about unworthiness, guilt, punishment, and sacrifice

Out of the past and future, to the place of now. Right to the center—to desire. To the place where I was free to choose again. And I desired peace, regardless of the body's condition.

Over the next few weeks, my experience of pain slowly disappeared. It was gone! Never to return.

So, what happened?

In the holy instant, which is the abode of miracles, all my past stories and grievances about the pain were simply erased. These stories included my experience with the pain, all I had done to heal the pain, all those who had tried but were unable to help me, and so on and so forth. It felt like deleting an old outdated cumbersome program from a computer that was taking a ton of space yet was no longer helpful. With this past suddenly deleted, there was empty space that could be filled with love—a rush of fresh energy that allowed for a whole new way to perceive.

Principle 13 of the principles of miracles section describes my experience perfectly:

> *Miracles are both beginnings and endings, and so they alter the temporal order. They are always affirmations of rebirth, which seem to go back but really go forward. They undo the past in the present, and thus release the future.*

It was completely counterintuitive. When I took my mind off the pain, it slowly disappeared.

All my training thus far had been completely the opposite: to analyze, dissect, and examine all symptoms of the body, including pain, from every possible angle. Usually this meant studying the *past* to heal in the *future*.

Yet the miracle doesn't exist in the past or the future. The miracle exists in the now. It allows a radical shift in awareness where we join with *what is* from a state of pure acceptance. No clinging, no pushing away. In this miracle of surrender, I discovered the healing that had eluded me for years. Soon this experience would open the doors to the deeper way of healing that I had searched for since my medical school days.

PART FOUR

Discovering Coaching for Inner Peace

CHAPTER 17

The Birth of Coaching for Inner Peace

The peace of God is everything I want. The peace of God is my one goal; the aim of all my living here, the end I seek, my purpose and my function and my life, while I abide where I am not at home.

After the fistula pain disappeared in June 2014, I still needed to negotiate another key decision: whether to undergo a surgical procedure that required general anesthesia. My surgeon informed me this surgery was needed for permanent resolution of the fistula. It was an ambulatory procedure so barring any complication, I would go home the same day. However, I would need to take off a few weeks from work for full recovery.

I felt great resistance to the surgery. My mind rushed to past experiences with the initial procedure in 2008. Could I trust my surgeon again? The first surgery was not a complete success so why would the second surgery be different? Since I felt no pain, I was even more reluctant and kept postponing the date. I knew as a physician that the mindset of a patient is a key factor in the success (or failure) of any operation, large or small. If I decided for surgery, I wanted to be on board 100%. So, I journaled and reflected about my fears and doubts and I joined in more heart-to-heart conversations with other mighty companions. One of my ACIM mentors helped me see that the surgery was a part of my inner wisdom's plan for my healing and my highest good. This helped me feel less fearful and more open. Gradually, I realized that avoiding the operation was like running away and allowing my ego mind to make my healing plans, rather than listening and following inner guidance.

Once I made a decision for surgery, everything fell into place seamlessly. At work, I received almost a month of paid medical leave. My parents flew in from New York City to support me in my healing and also to help care for my son. In addition, unlike my feelings prior to the first surgery, I felt an unmistakable and peaceful clarity.

The only place I felt any responsibility was at the level of the mind. I opened to fully accept the surgery as a given—as a part of my inner guide's plan for healing. The only true choice I could make was about the purpose. What purpose would this experience serve?

I was determined to not let the ego mind take over, to teach me about suffering, pain, sacrifice, guilt, or punishment. Regardless of the outer play of events, I would not allow myself to play the poor sick martyr role. I was done with that. The only purpose was healing of my mind. I trusted that everything would be taken care of by my inner guide. With this decision at the forefront of my mind, I surrendered gracefully to the experience.

Receiving a Healed Perception

On the morning of the surgery, I still felt peaceful. My son was at summer camp, so I could focus on my healing. My mom helped me with the bowel prep, which went smoothly. My dad then drove my mom and me to the surgical office. The nurse who greeted us appeared like an angel to me. As soon as she smiled at me, I felt I was in good hands. Even the IV insertion flowed effortlessly.

My hospital stretcher was near a window draped with lovely sea-green curtains. In the background, the hospital speakers serenaded me with some of my favorite songs—the *Happy* song by Pharrell, and the *Greased Lightning* song with John Travolta. The playlist seemed to have been created especially for me! As I leaned back and enjoyed the music, the nurse admired my salmon pink manicure and pedicure, a gift of self-care I had purposely pampered myself with the day before. If I had to have surgery and wear a hospital gown, I could still do it in style!

While waiting for the surgery to begin, I felt tears of gratitude well up in my eyes. Yes, I was lying on a hospital stretcher awaiting surgery. Yet I felt grounded in serenity and surrounded by beauty. I felt such love and peace. I knew that my inner guide was with me every step of the way. I could not help but smile sheepishly to myself. So, this is what I was resisting all this time? This amazing experience of being held in the arms of love? How silly of me!

Soon my surgeon arrived to escort me into a different room. Initially, I felt a slight ripple of fear. The new room was windowless and appeared more hospital-sterile than the pre-surgical suite with sea-green curtains, music, and beauty. Yet I recall that this fear was followed by a calm inner voice that assured me: *You are going deeper into your mind for healing, but you are still safe. Don't get distracted by the external appearance. Reach deeper into the mind for love. You are okay.*

The last thing I recall is a conversation with the nurse anesthesiologist about my sensitivity to anesthesia. I suggested she start with half the normal amount and increase if necessary. The next thing I remember is being back in the room with the sea-green curtains, once more held in love, beauty and serenity. I was surrounded by my parents, the surgeon, the nurse, and a few other surgical team members. There was no fear, only love.

The surgeon remarked that he was surprised to discover the fistula site had *already* healed so the surgical repair needed was less than anticipated. He was happy with the results and wanted to see me again in a month. I was still under the effects of anesthesia, but I didn't feel groggy or nauseous. I felt a sense of being light and held in light and love. Everything felt illumined.

When I arrived home after the procedure, I continued to feel a sense of peace, safety and ease. I was prescribed some codeine-containing pain medications. In the past, however, I had experienced reactions to the codeine, so I decided to stick with over the counter medications for pain. My mind felt no resistance to such medications or that I should take something more natural. Overall, I felt very little pain but if I experienced even slight discomfort, I took the medicine and didn't try to tough it out. My mind was in a dramatically different place from where it was after the first surgery. I simply cared for myself in the way that felt most loving and helpful—letting myself rest, taking medications as I felt guided, and allowing my parents and others to help me as needed.

A month later when I checked in with my surgeon, not only was he pleased with the healing, but he was also impressed that I needed so little pain medication. After our first appointment, he discharged me from his care. I felt so much healing with respect to judgments about surgery, surgeons, anesthesia, and medications; my resistance had vanished. If the surgeon had asked me to come again for follow-up, that would have been fine too. I felt a sense of peace and trust about the entire issue, with no need to control anything. I *knew* my inner guide was in charge and I was safe.

The Healing Power of Forgiveness

The events of the second surgery felt like a beautiful cascade of miracles. They were a stark contrast to my previous experience in 2008 when everything seemed to go wrong — from the preoperative bowel preparation, to the IV insertion, to the postoperative recovery from anesthesia. Afterward, I also experienced a difficult postoperative course with much pain.

Given what I understand about healing today, I know that these side effects reflected my own inner resistance to these procedures. I was caught in judgments about surgeons, surgery, anesthesia, and medications. I believed these were not natural and thus bad, whereas herbal medications, homeopathy, yoga, Reiki, and meditation were all natural and good. I believed I knew the way my healing should happen, so the surgery in 2008 felt like a huge failure. We could say that I was in a state of separation or unforgiveness.

The miracle awoke my sleeping mind to see correctly so I could perceive my situation from a different perspective. Before, I had viewed my experience through the lens of fear and judgment. Now, however, the inner process of radical forgiveness allowed me to see through a completely different lens. Even with the same history of pain, the same surgeon and a similar surgical procedure, my experience was entirely different because my perception was different. From my healed perception, the outer healing of my body followed naturally. In addition, I was now convinced that healing could be inclusive, using tools such as surgery, anesthesia, and pain medications along with prayer, meditation, journaling, heart-to-heart discussions with trustworthy companions, and support from family and friends.

Healing Is the Acceptance of Inner Peace

During the months following my surgery, I continued to feel peaceful and pain-free. Yet I felt a growing restlessness at my job where I worked with patients suffering from chronic emotional and/or physical pain seeking disability benefits. I was hired to document their disability in detail but not make any determination with respect to their eligibility for disability benefits or offer any treatment. I wanted to share a new way to heal that was deep, broad, and profound and that was based on my own experience. However, I couldn't do this at this job and I felt no desire to find another traditional medical job or to go back to practicing integrative/holistic medicine.

I recall having a conversation about this with my friend and teacher, David Hoffmeister, who suggested that if I could give up the form of what I felt my career should look like, I would find it. I took David's words to heart. I let go of trying to figure things out. Instead each day before going to work, I allowed myself time to meditate, reflect, and journal.

Gradually, I began to receive new insights. I recalled my experience of utter stillness and peace within the cave in northern India the summer before I entered medical school. I also realized that this was the peace I felt when I was present at my dad's recovery and healing from the gunshot wound. It was the same peace and sense of comfort and safety that pervaded my entire experience of my recent surgery. This peace was not due to anything external. It seemed to just emanate from me and surround me like a protective yet porous cocoon. I felt sheltered and safe inside, yet at the same time, I felt a genuine ability to connect to others around me.

I had studied about relaxation and the stress response, which we reviewed in chapter 3. Although relaxation was certainly part of it, this feeling of inner peace was much more. To me, experiencing inner peace felt like coming home, but this home had nothing to do with any physical location, what the body was doing, or even whether the body was sick. My experience had taught me that *inner peace came first and then the healing followed*—not the other way around.

To discover inner peace amidst suffering of the body and/or the mind was no easy task. I knew it required much willingness on my part and help from countless mighty companions. It also required being exposed to a radically different way to think about everything and everyone in my life.

A Systematic Way to Heal

During this time, a former client, Jane,[104] from my integrative practice, contacted me. She was distraught, on the edge of spiraling into a deep depression associated with a recent break-up. I listened deeply as she poured out her heart.

That evening, as I reflected on the challenges facing Jane, a light bulb went off inside my head. I realized that Jane was one among many facing a life-altering situation that left them feeling helpless, powerless, depressed, and fearful.

For Jane, her life seemed to be falling apart. Yet because I knew her for many years, I could see that it was this break-up that had cracked her heart wide open. If given the purpose of deep, transformative healing, could this same pain serve Jane as the catalyst for a quantum leap in her ability to give and receive love? As Buddhist teacher Pema Chodron says, when our life is falling apart, this can be a fertile opportunity to *fall together* in a new way.[105]

What if Jane were offered a step-by-step program that supported her to use this painful challenge as a substrate to fuel deep healing? We know that a steady spring rain leaves the ground smelling fresh, renewed, and revitalized. Could an ongoing structured program that supported Jane during this acutely painful time serve a similar nurturing and healing purpose? What would such a program look like? What would be the steps one would need to take?

I knew the program needed to be systematic but not rigid, simple yet not simplistic. It also needed to be expansive, integrative, and holistic. This meant the outer and inner journey needed to come together. For example, for Jane, her inner emotional journey of fear, guilt, sadness, and self-doubt needed to be honored and integrated with her outer experience of her recent break-up and its effects on her overall health and well-being. Finally, it was essential that this program empower Jane by teaching her to connect with her deep inner resources. This way, she could learn to listen to her inner wisdom while negotiating the external path of working with other health care professionals and therapists.

That evening, I received a clear roadmap of Coaching for Inner Peace. I didn't *try* to write this down with my logical, left-brain mind. Rather, I saw all the steps of the program in one flash of inspiration. Over the next few months, I wrote, rewrote, and revised what my inner wisdom was sharing with me. Amazingly, these were the same steps I had used for my own healing!

CHAPTER 18

A Pathway of Miracles

Miracles reawaken the awareness that the spirit, not the body,
is the altar of truth. This is the recognition that leads to the
healing power of the miracle.

Fulfilling My Destiny

Ever since entering medical school, I had been searching for a
way to heal that would unite the Eastern with the Western,
the traditional with the complementary, and the inner with
the outer. I envisioned that the parts of each discipline that
currently seemed isolated or separate would merge into a
beautiful whole with inner peace at the center.

I was also eager to incorporate what I had learned during my
own healing journey into a viable program that could be
effective for many others as well as myself. By integrating the
inner journey of the mind—our emotions, fears and doubts—
with the outer path of pain, illness, and medical care, and by
incorporating ACIM into a program I named Coaching for
Inner Peace, I felt I was on the way to fulfilling my destiny.

Coaching for Inner Peace is a bridge we can traverse with
confidence as we attend to the whole, leaving no parts of our
experience behind. In this chapter I will share with you the
template of Coaching for Inner Peace to support your journey
of healing.

Asking Questions

When we find ourselves witnessing pain and suffering in the world around us or experiencing it ourselves, often we question why this is happening. Why did this cancer happen to me? Why does my child, or parent or partner or friend, have to go through this pain? In my personal and professional experience, I have discovered that asking questions is a powerful way to engage our inner resources for healing. However, it's important we ask questions that yield productive answers—questions that come from a space of nonjudgment and nonresistance. *Why* questions are unlikely to be helpful—they usually compound our sense of feeling powerless and helpless because they rarely lead us to satisfactory answers. Instead, we want to cultivate a sense of curiosity as we engage in our experience with an open mind and open heart.

The following are some questions that can invite a more expansive way to relate to our experience.

Am I Willing?

In order to heal, we must first be willing to accept where we are. This may sound obvious yet when we face a challenging situation, our first reaction is often one of resistance. We may wish that the cancer or illness or whatever emotional or physical pain we are facing would simply go away. We may frantically search for a solution outside of ourselves to release our pain. Even if we consider ourselves spiritual individuals or healers with a spiritual practice, we may still wish for a shortcut. We may be pleading, *Just give me a miracle so I don't have to go deeper and face my pain within my mind and heart!*

From this space, we can often spiral into panic, anger, or even depression. We may blame our body for failing us, our loved one for deserting us, the doctor for misdiagnosing us, or even God or the universe for abandoning and somehow betraying us.

In this stance of resistance, willingness is like a candle that can illumine the darkness of our minds. It is an acknowledgment that even if we don't know how to move forward, we are willing to lean into our not-knowing and allow for a deeper knowing from our inner wisdom to emerge. We are willing to simply show up, even if we don't know how it will all work out.

Willingness Is at the Heart of Commitment

When we embark on a healing program, we are often asked to make a commitment to complete the course of treatment or therapy. However, the word commitment can often provoke anxiety and a sense of pressure; it can feel heavy and burdensome because often it is intertwined with a sense of personal responsibility. If we are not successful in our commitment, then we might feel guilty because we somehow failed. We may find it difficult if not impossible to even take the first step. That is why I love the word willingness, which is a fundamental part of ACIM. Interestingly, the online English Cambridge dictionary defines commitment as "a willingness to give your time and energy to something you believe in."[106]

Being willing simply means we are open to show up and be present. We are not trying to push this circumstance away *and* we're not running away either. We are simply willing to show up as we are, how we are, with whatever resources we have or don't have. In my coaching practice, the clients I work with feel great relief right after the first session because I am not asking them to do more, or fix something, or even change themselves. Rather, I invite them to move into a space of willingness where they can breathe and simply be. Can you feel the openness and expansiveness of this state of mind?

What Is My Desire? What Do I Truly Want?

Being willing is a wonderful first step. Yet what is this willingness for? What is our desire? What do we really want? From coaching hundreds of clients, I know life can bring us many different challenges, ranging from illness to grief to relationship conflicts as well as the associated emotional and mental stress. The *form* of our problems or challenges can vary immensely. However, the *content* we all seek is essentially the same: to feel happy, safe, loved, and at peace. Instead of trying to fix the form of our problems, I invite my clients to first sit with this profound realization that whatever solution we seek outside is essentially a desire for an experience of love, peace, and joy.

What Is My Purpose?

When I work with my clients, regardless of the form of their outer challenge, my purpose is always the same. The goal is to develop a way to heal that brings parts that seem isolated or separate into a beautiful whole with inner peace at the center.

First, however, before we can even begin the healing process, we must be willing to view our present circumstances differently. The caterpillar emerges as a beautiful butterfly from the darkness of the chrysalis. Healing and transformation often emerge from deep distress and despair. No matter how bleak and difficult our challenge may appear on the outside, we need to be willing to join with our inner wisdom to give our circumstances the deeper purpose of healing our minds.[107]

How Can I Forgive the Obstacles to Healing?

When we open to healing our minds, often we encounter both external and internal obstacles. I share with my clients that the process of healing our minds can at first feel like washing a load of dirty dishes after a holiday dinner. Things are going to get dirty before they get clean. Often, the pain we experience—even if it shows up on the physical plane within our bodies—reflects painful, deeply buried emotions. In our culture, we have many ways to distract or numb ourselves when we feel pain—television, movies, the Internet, social media, food, drugs, work, relationships, sex, shopping, and so forth. Even our spiritual practice can be misused by the ego mind to create a spiritual by-pass and thus divert our attention from pain (see chapter 15). Yet often we do not have safe spaces where we can truly be with our pain and allow for the healing.

When I invite clients to look at the pain they hold within themselves as they negotiate a physical illness, emotional trauma, or some other life transition, I am clear with them that the purpose is not to get stuck or lost in stories of guilt, blame, shame, or loss. Rather, it is to allow the process of forgiveness to wash away the residue of past hurts so we can experience a new way to relate to life.

How Can I Connect with My Inner Wisdom and Join More Deeply with Others?

Within ourselves, we have all the answers we need for negotiating any challenge we face. Yet the process of looking inside is often not our natural way of operating in the world. Since our eyes look outward, literally as well as metaphorically, we need help to look at ourselves and go within. In addition, from a very young age, we become habituated to understand ourselves based on our achievements and possessions in the outer world. We constantly chase outward accolades—having the perfect body, finding the perfect career, being in the perfect relationship, living in the perfect home, finding the perfect school system for our children—and the list continues.

ACIM teaches that even illness is some form of external searching. How often do we fill our calendars with more and more activities, ultimately preventing us from being still and going within? Perhaps some of us are even vaguely aware that within ourselves we carry a dark void that feels so huge and overwhelming in its enormity, we dare not go within because we fear the annihilation of our very existence. Frantically we try to fill this seemingly bottomless and excruciatingly painful sense of hollowness with activities and busyness from the outside.

Like Dorothy in *The Wizard of Oz*, we have the power to return home, to a place of safety, rest, peace, joy, and love. Yet this usually cannot occur until we take our hero's journey where we must meet and forgive our inner dragons and demons.

Who can help us here? What do we have within us that can serve as a trustworthy guide as we walk this inner journey? We need to not only find a way to connect to our deepest inner wisdom, but we also need help and support from our mighty companions.

Dorothy begins her journey to Oz on her own but soon she is joined by the Scarecrow, the Tin Man, and the Cowardly Lion.

Each is seeking something outside themselves to feel whole. Yet by joining in a common purpose to meet the Wizard together, each discovers that the very thing they sought was right inside them all the time.

How Can I Surrender and Let Go?

One of the most profound teachings of ACIM is to cultivate the willingness to surrender and trust in our inner wisdom and allow this wisdom to lead our way—to do this again, and again, and yet again, because this is the only way to experience inner peace.

Most of us are familiar with the famous Serenity Prayer.[108]

God, grant me the serenity to accept the things I cannot change, courage to change the things I can, and wisdom to know the difference.

This is a beautiful prayer of acceptance and surrender, which does not mean we become immobilized or frozen. If we truly practice the teachings of the Serenity Prayer, we see that the process of surrender is not about being powerless, passive, and helpless; rather, it is the complete opposite. Surrender is an active choice we make from a place of peace and trust. We lean into love instead of clinging to fear. We learn to exercise our power of choice which lies in our capacity to change our minds, our attitudes, beliefs, and perceptions. At the same time, we learn to accept the given—the circumstances of our challenge that we cannot change. Finally, surrender is a dynamic, evolving journey where we learn to listen deeply to our inner guide to help us discern with clarity again and again—where we have choice and where we do not.

How Can I Let Go of the Form of the Outcome?

What about situations in which the body passes on? Or when the healing seems not to happen and the pain continues, whether in the body, mind, or both? It is precisely in these situations that the practice of surrender is essential. Surrender is a willingness to open again and again to see our circumstances differently so we may reconnect with peace. *Our focus is not on the external outcome but on the experience of inner peace.*

I firmly believe there is a happy dream of forgiveness and miracles for remedying each challenge of pain, sorrow, or loss that we face. Our story is not done until we experience the soothing balm of love in a way that leaves us feeling healed and whole.

However, it takes great humility to realize that often we don't know what the form of healing may look like, or the optimal path for allowing this healing in ourselves or another. That is why an active and consistent process of deep listening to our inner wisdom is essential. We also need to be willing to allow our inner wisdom to purify and clear all our concepts, judgments, and beliefs about our experience. As we open to a new perspective, if there are action steps we need to take to support our healing or that of another, we are guided so we can be truly helpful.

On the surface it may appear that to surrender is to somehow give up and lose something of value, such as control over an outcome. However, this is not the case at all. When we surrender, we join our small will with the divine will. We allow ourselves to be lifted above the battlefield of conflict, confusion, and complexity to a state of peace, love, and joy.

From this space, miracles flow forth not *because* of our doing but rather *despite* our doing.

The key to healing is *to get out of our own way and not interfere.* This is the essence of surrender. This is the timeless wisdom and beauty of the Serenity Prayer—to allow our inner guide to act through us. Then, to let ourselves be taken care of completely and perfectly in ways that we simply cannot even imagine, let alone plan or control with our logical, everyday thinking mind.

With a deepening practice of surrender, we not only loosen our attempt to control external outcomes, but we also open to a more expansive vision of life. We have a body, yet we are not the body. We inhabit this physical form, yet we are much more than the physical. Our truth is so vast that even the immenseness of the ocean and the star-filled night sky are mere specks of dust in comparison. We are infinite wisdom, infinite energy, infinite light, and infinite love.

A Pathway of Miracles: Being Lifted Out of Time

In this book we have explored many different tools and practices to help us heal—movies, meditation, music, mind watching, mind training, metaphysics, mythology, prayer, journaling, forgiveness, gratitude, and joining. By applying these tools and practices, little by little, step by step, we can shift our perception of and identification with the body, so we can rest in our true nature.

We are lifted above the laws of the world so that even the awareness of our body and our challenge can slowly recede from our minds. In this full and total experience of the present moment, we step out of time into the timeless and taste the eternal. Healing can occur in this instant, just as it did for me in a cave in northern India. Yet often the playing out of this healing *in time* can seem to *take time.*

To allow healing, we need to become time travelers. We master the art of being *in* this world but not *of* this world. We learn to step out of time, even if briefly, to connect to the space of stillness from where we literally download information. This information can be in the form of inspired ideas, images, music, or other insights that provide us with a different way to understand and relate to our lives. Or it may simply be a broadcast of love, comfort, and peace. We then return to the present to further assimilate this information and then, as we feel guided, we share and extend these divine downloads to others in our social circle of family, friends, and colleagues. We trust in our inner guide to orchestrate all things to ultimately work together for the highest good of everyone.

A Prayer from the Heart

I thank you from the depths of my heart for your willingness to accompany my dearest Papa and Mom, and me, on our journey from a small hospital in northern India to the writing of this book.

Wherever you are, whatever challenge you may be facing, please know that from across the distance of space and time, we join with you in the mighty purpose of healing. May this book bless you along your path. May it offer you comfort and solace when you lose hope. May it serve as a beacon of light when you feel lost and confused. And finally, may it remind you that you are always entitled to miracles simply because you are, always have been, and always will be a beloved and cherished child of God.

Namaste.

ACIM Notes

Preface

ACIM C-In.2:5: A universal theology is impossible, but a universal experience is not only possible but necessary.

Introduction

ACIM T-21.I.7:5: Listen, and see if you remember an ancient song you knew so long ago and held more dear than any melody you taught yourself to cherish since.

Chapter 1

ACIM W-pI.32: I have invented the world I see.

Chapter 2

ACIM W-pI.2: I have given everything I see... all the meaning that it has for me.

Chapter 3

ACIM T-13.V.10:1-2: You have but two emotions, and one you made and one was given you. Each is a way of seeing, and different worlds arise from their different sights.

Chapter 4

ACIM W-pI.155.2:1-6: The world is an illusion. Those who choose to come to it are seeking for a place where they can be illusions, and avoid their own reality. Yet when they find their own reality is even here, then they step back and let it lead the way. What other choice is really theirs to make? To let illusions walk ahead of truth is madness. But to let illusion sink behind the truth and let the truth stand forth as what it is, is merely sanity.

ACIM T-21.1.8:1-6: Beyond the body, beyond the sun and stars, past everything you see and yet somehow familiar, is an arc of golden light that stretches as you look into a great and shining circle. And all the circle fills with light before your eyes. The edges of the circle disappear, and what is in it is no longer contained at all. The light expands and covers everything, extending to infinity forever shining and with no break or limit anywhere. Within it everything is joined in perfect continuity. Nor is it possible to imagine that anything could be outside, for there is nowhere that this light is not.

ACIM T-18.IX.4:1: The circle of fear lies just below the level the body sees, and seems to be the whole foundation on which the world is based.

ACIM In-4: The purpose of the workbook is to train your mind in a systematic way to a different perception of everyone and everything in the world.

Chapter 5

ACIM W-pI.60.1:4: Yet forgiveness is the means by which I will recognize my innocence.

Chapter 6

ACIM W-pI.121: Forgiveness is the key to happiness.

ACIM T-21.II.2:3-5: I **am** responsible for what I see. I choose the feelings I experience, and I decide upon the goal I would achieve. And everything that seems to happen to me I ask for, and receive as I have asked.

Chapter 7

ACIM W-pI.33: There is another way of looking at the world.

Chapter 8

ACIM T-5.II.7:1-2,4-7: The Voice of the Holy Spirit does not command, because It is incapable of arrogance. It does not demand, because It does not seek control... It merely reminds. It is compelling only because of what It reminds you *of*. It brings to your mind the other way, remaining quiet even in the midst of the turmoil you may make. The Voice for God is always quiet, because It speaks of peace.

Chapter 9

ACIM W-p1.169.2.1-2: Grace is acceptance of the Love of God within a world of seeming hate and fear. By grace alone the hate and fear are gone, for grace presents a state so opposite to everything the world contains, that those whose minds are lighted by the gift of grace can not believe the world of fear is real.

Chapter 10

ACIM W-p1.76.6.1: There are no laws except the laws of God.

ACIM W-p1.195.2.1-2; 195.9: It is insane to offer thanks because of suffering. But it is equally insane to fail in gratitude to One Who offers you the certain means whereby all pain is healed, and suffering replaced with laughter and with happiness... Today we learn to think of gratitude in place of anger, malice and revenge.

ACIM W-p1.76.9.3: You will be listening to One Who says there is no loss under the laws of God.

Chapter 11

ACIM W-p1.201.4-6: I am not a body. I am free. For I am still as God created me.

ACIM T-28.II.12:1-2: This world is full of miracles. They stand in shining silence next to every dream of pain and suffering, of sin and guilt.

Chapter 12

ACIM T-17.VI.2:1-3: In any situation in which you are uncertain, the first thing to consider, very simply, is "What do I want to come of this? What is it *for*?" The clarification of the goal belongs at the beginning, for it is this which will determine the outcome.

Chapter 13

ACIM T-1.I.3:1-3: Miracles occur naturally as expressions of love. The real miracle is the love that inspires them. In this sense everything that comes from love is a miracle.

ACIM T-1.I.1:1-4: There is no order of difficulty in miracles. One is not "harder" or "bigger" than another. They are all the same. All expressions of love are maximal.

Chapter 14

ACIM M-29.2:6-7: The curriculum is highly individualized, and all aspects are under the Holy Spirit's particular care and guidance. Ask and He will answer.

ACIM T-18.V.1:5-6: Put yourself not in charge of this, for you cannot distinguish between advance and retreat. Some of your greatest advances you have judged as failures, and some of your deepest retreats you have evaluated as success.

ACIM T-1.1.7: Miracles are everyone's right, but purification is necessary first.

Chapter 15

ACIM T-13.III.6:1,4-5: You must look upon your illusions and not keep them hidden, because they do not rest on their own foundation.... For beneath them, and concealed as long as they are hidden, is the loving mind that thought it made them in anger. And the pain in this mind is so apparent, when it is uncovered, that its need of healing cannot be denied.

ACIM T-2.II.2:1 True denial is a powerful protective device.

ACIM W-pI.8 My mind is preoccupied with past thoughts.

ACIM W-pI.71.9: 3-5 What would You have me do? Where would You have me go? What would You have me say, and to whom?

ACIM-T-28.III.2:6 Healing is the effect of minds that join, as sickness comes from minds that separate.

Chapter 16

ACIM T-1.I.17:1-3 Miracles transcend the body. They are sudden shifts into invisibility, away from the bodily level. That is why they heal.

ACIM T-2.IV.2:2 Sickness or "not right-mindedness" is the result of level confusion, because it always entails the belief that what is amiss on one level can adversely affect another.

ACIM T-2.I.5:11 Health is inner peace.

ACIM T-2.IV.4:1-10 All material means that you accept as remedies for bodily ills are restatements of magic principles. This is the first step in believing that the body makes its own illness. It is a second misstep to attempt to heal it through non-creative agents. It does not follow, however, that the use of such agents for corrective purposes is evil. Sometimes the illness has a sufficiently strong hold over the mind to render a person temporarily inaccessible to the Atonement. In this case it may be wise to utilize a compromise approach to mind and body, in which something from the outside is temporarily given healing belief. This is because the last thing that can help the non-right-minded, or the sick, is an increase in fear. They are already in a fear-weakened state. If they are prematurely exposed to a miracle, they may be precipitated into panic. This is likely to occur when upside-down perception has induced the belief that miracles are frightening.

ACIM T-16.VII.6:4-6 In the holy instant it is understood that the past is gone... The stillness and the peace of *now* enfold you in perfect gentleness. Everything is gone except the truth.

ACIM T-1.I.13:1-3 Miracles are both beginnings and endings, and so they alter the temporal order. They are always affirmations of rebirth, which seem to go back but really go forward. They undo the past in the present, and thus release the future.

Chapter 17

ACIM W-pI.205.2-3 The peace of God is everything I want. The peace of God is my one goal; the aim of all my living here, the end I seek, my purpose and my function and my life, while I abide where I am not at home.

Chapter 18

ACIM T-1.I.20:1-2 Miracles reawaken the awareness that the spirit, not the body, is the altar of truth. This is the recognition that leads to the healing power of the miracle.

Notes

Introduction

[1] Ayurveda is a science of life (Ayur = life, Veda = science or knowledge). The two main guiding principles of Ayurveda are 1) the mind and the body are inextricably connected, and 2) nothing has more power to heal and transform the body than the mind. Chopra, Deepak. "What is Ayurveda?" The Chopra Center, chopra.com/articles/what-is-ayurveda

[2] When I refer to mind, I include our thoughts, beliefs, emotions, perceptions as well as our desires—both conscious and subconscious.

Chapter 1

[3] Darshan is derived from the Sanskrit word for "viewing" or "vision" of a deity, saint, or other revered person or sacred object. In Hinduism, this is believed to result in the flowing of a blessing to the human viewer. "Darshan." Ananda: Joy Is Within You, ananda.org/yogapedia/darshan/

Chapter 2

[4] Feinberg, Cara. "The placebo phenomenon." *Harvard Magazine* (Jan – Feb 2013). 36-39, harvardmagazine.com/2013/01/the-placebo-phenomenon

[5] DeCraen, Anton J.M., Ted J. Kaptchuk, Jan G.P. Tijssen and J. Kleijnen. "Placebos and placebo effects in medicine: historical overview." *Journal of the Royal Society of Medicine* 92(1999).511-15, ncbi.nlm.nih.gov/pmc/articles/PMC1297390/pdf/jrsocmed00004-0023.pdf

[6] Beecher, Henry K. "The powerful placebo." *JAMA* 159(1955).1602-6, dcscience.net/beecher-placebo-1955.pdf

[7] Dispenza, Joe. You are the placebo: making your mind matter.

[8] Beecher, Henry K. "The powerful placebo."

[9] Dispenza, Joe. You are the placebo: making your mind matter.

[10] Klopfer, B. "Psychological variables in human cancer." *Journal of Projective Techniques and Personality Assessment.*21, no. 4(1957).331-40, tandfonline.com/doi/abs/10.1080/08853126.1957.10380794

[11] DeCraen, Anton J.M., Ted J. Kaptchuk, Jan G.P. Tijssen and J. Kleijnen. "Placebos and placebo effects in medicine: historical overview."

[12] Klopfer, B. "Psychological variables in human cancer."

[13] Ibid.

[14] Ibid.

[15] Ibid.

[16] Ibid.

[17] Ibid.

[18] Ibid.

[19] Ibid.

[20] Ibid.

[21] Ikemi, Yujiro and Shunji Nakagawa. "A Psychosomatic study of contagious dermatitis." *Kyoshu Journal of Medical Science* 13, no. 6 (1962).335-50, eurekamag.com/ftext.php?pdf=029759605

[22] Kirsch, Irving. "Response expectancy as a determinant of experience and behavior." *American Psychologist* 40, no. 11 (1985). 1189-1202, psycnet.apa.org/doiLanding?doi=10.1037%2F0003-066X.40.11.1189

[23] Kirsch, Irving and Guy Sapirstein. "Listening to Prozac but hearing placebo: A meta-analysis of antidepressant medication." Prevention & Treatment 1, no.2 (1998). Article ID 2a, dx.doi.org/10.1037/1522-3736.1.1.12a

[24] Kirsch, Irving, Thomas J. Moore, Alan Scoboria and Sarah S. Nicholls. "The emperor's new drugs: An analysis of antidepressant medication data submitted to the U.S. Food and Drug Administration." *Prevention and Treatment,* 5, no. 23(2002), researchgate.net/publication/228550299

[25] Cobb, Leonard A., George I. Thomas, David H. Dillard, K. Alvin Merendino, and Robert A. Bruce, M.D. "An Evaluation of Internal-Mammary-Artery Ligation by a Double-Blind Technic." *New England Journal of Medicine,* 260 (1959).1115- 1118, nejm.org/doi/full/10.1056/NEJM195905282602204

[26] Stolberg, Sheryl Gay. "Ideas & Trends; Sham Surgery Returns as a Research Tool." *The New York Times.* April 25, 1999, nytimes.com/1999/04/25/weekinreview/ideas-trends-sham-surgery-returns-as-a-research-tool.html

[27] Moseley, J. Bruce, Kimberly O'Malley, Nancy J. Petersen, Terri J. Menke, Baruch A. Brody, David H. Kuykendall, John C. Hollingsworth, Carol M. Ashton, and Nelda P. Wray. "A Controlled Trial of Arthroscopic Surgery for Osteoarthritis of the Knee." *New England Journal of Medicine,* 347(2002).81-88, nejm.org/doi/full/10.1056/NEJMoa013259#t=article

[28] Sihvonen, Raine, Mika Paavola, Antti Malmivaara, Ari Itälä, Antti Joukainen, Heikki Nurmi, Juha Kalske and Teppo L.N. Järvinen for the Finnish Degenerative Meniscal Lesion Study (FIDELITY) Group. "Arthroscopic Partial Meniscectomy versus Sham Surgery for a

Degenerative Meniscal Tear." *New England Journal of Medicine*, 369(2013).2515-2524, nejm.org/doi/full/10.1056/NEJMoa1305189#t=article

[29] Kaptchuk, Ted J., Elizabeth Friedlander, John M. Kelley, M. Norma Sanchez, Efi Kokkotou, Joyce P. Singer, Magda Kowalczykowski, Franklin G. Miller, Irving Kirsch and Anthony J. Lembo "Placebo without deception: a randomized controlled trial in irritable bowel syndrome." *PLoS One*, 5, no.12 (2010). e15591, ncbi.nlm.nih.gov/pmc/articles/PMC3008733

Chapter 3

[30] "The Center for Mind Body Medicine Mission." Center for Mind-Body Medicine, cmbm.org/about/mission/

[31] "Understanding the stress response: Chronic activation of this survival mechanism impairs health." Harvard Health Publishing: Harvard Medical School. March 2011. Updated May 1, 2018, health.harvard.edu/staying-healthy/understanding-the-stress-response

[32] "Understanding the stress response: Chronic activation of this survival mechanism impairs health." Harvard Health Publishing: Harvard Medical School.

[33] Sargis, Robert M. "An Overview of the Hypothalamus: The Endocrine System's Link to the Nervous System." Endocrine Web, endocrineweb.com/endocrinology/overview-hypothalamus

[34] "Understanding the stress response: Chronic activation of this survival mechanism impairs health." Harvard Health Publishing: Harvard Medical School.

[35] Porter, James. "How can you explain a PTSD "trigger" to someone who isn't familiar with PTSD?" StressStop.com: Stress Management Training that Works. Published November 30, 2018, stressstop.com/blogs/ask-jim/how-can-you-explain-a-ptsd-trigger-to-someone-who-isnt-familiar-with-ptsd

[36] Salleh, Mohd. Razali. "Life Event, Stress and Illness." *Malaysian Journal of Medical* Sciences 15, no. 4 (2008). 9–18, ncbi.nlm.nih.gov/pmc/articles/PMC3341916/

[37] Kirby, Stephanie. "Chronic Stress: How It Affects You And How To Get Relief." Better Help. Updated November 13, 2019, betterhelp.com/advice/stress/chronic-stress-how-it-affects-you-and-how-to-get-relief/

[38] Dispenza, Joe. *You are the placebo: making your mind matter*. Carlsbad: Hay House, 2014, amazon.com/dp/1401944582

[39] Emory, Margaret. "Tracking the Mind-Body Connection: An Interview with Dr. Herbert Benson." Brain World. Published December 18, 2018, brainworldmagazine.com/dr-herbert-benson-on-the-mindbody-connection/

[40] Mitchell, Marilyn. "Dr. Herbert Benson's Relaxation Response: Learn to counteract the physiological effects of stress." Heart and Soul Healing, Psychology Today. Published Mar 29, 2013, psychologytoday.com/blog/heart-and-soul-healing/201303/dr-herbert-benson-s-relaxation-response

[41] Emory, Margaret. "Tracking the Mind-Body Connection: An Interview with Dr. Herbert Benson."

[42] In the clarification of terms in *A Course in Miracles*, this is referred to as *right-mindedness* and *wrong-mindedness*. Right-mindedness listens to the voice for peace and love, while wrong-mindedness listens to the voice of ego. (C- 1.5:2; C-1.6:1) Some of my clients have stated that the terms *right* and *wrong* can invoke a sense of self-judgment or judgment about others. So, I have chosen to refer to the two ways the mind can perceive using different terms. The meaning is still the same as shared in the teachings of ACIM.

[43] Kraft, Kenneth. *Zen: Tradition and Transition: A Sourcebook by Contemporary Zen Masters and Scholars*. New York: Grove Press, 1988, amazon.com/dp/080213162X

Chapter 4

[44] "Legends of Narada." Indian Divinity, webonautics.com/mythology/narada_legends5.html

[45] Schimmrich, Steven H. "The scale of atoms." Hudson Valley Geologist. Published December 31, 2011, hudsonvalleygeologist.blogspot.com/2011/12/scale-of-atoms.html

[46] Dispenza, Joe. *Becoming Supernatural: How Common People Are Doing the Uncommon*. Carlsbad: Hay House, 2017, amazon.com/dp/1401953093

[47] "An Exclusive Interview by Veronica M. Hay with Deepak Chopra."Okyanus: For brains that question and contemplate, okyanusum.com/en/?p=10513

[48] Ibid.

[49] Scholnick, Robert J. *American Literature and Science*. Kentucky: University Press of Kentucky, 1992, books. google.com/books?id=NbRk8AIjnP4C

[50] Ibid.

[51] Swami Rama. *Path of Fire and Light (Vol 2): A Practical Companion to Volume One (Volume 1)*. Honesdale: Himalayan Institute Press, 1988,

amazon.com/dp/0893891126

[52] Greshko, Michaeal. "Origins of the Universe 101." *National Geographic.* Published January 18, 2017, nationalgeographic.com/science/space/universe/origins-of-the-universe/

[53] Popova, Maria. "Einstein on Widening Our Circles of Compassion." Brain Pickings, brainpickings.org/2016/11/28/einstein-circles-of-compassion/

Chapter 5

[54] Swami Prabhavananda, Christopher Isherwood, and Aldous Huxley. *Bhagavad Gita: The Song of God.* New York: Signet Classic, 2002, amazon.com/dp/0451528441

[55] Shemaroo. "Jagte Raho - Jago Mohan Pyare - Lata Mangeshkar." YouTube video, 5:59. Posted (July 2010), youtu.be/_X0e5AS7EPw

[56] Jaago Mohan Pyare, Jaago lyrics from *Jagte Raho*, hindilyrics.net/lyrics/of-Jaago%20Mohan%20Pyare,%20Jaago.html

Chapter 6

[57] Vitale, Joe & Len, Hew Ihaleakala. *Zero Limits: The Secret Hawaiian System for Wealth, Health, Peace and More.* Hoboken: John Wiley & Sons, Inc., 2007, amazon.com/dp/0470402563

[58] Khalsa, Sita. "Morrnah Nalamaku Simeona, Hawaiian healer." Amazing Women in History. Published November 28, 2012, amazingwomeninhistory.com/morrnah-nalamaku-simeona-hawaiian-healer/

[59] Vitale, Joe & Len, Hew Ihaleakala. Zero Limits: The Secret Hawaiian System for Wealth, Health, Peace and More.

[60] Ibid.

[61] Russell, Peter. "Peter Russell- Biography." Peter Russell- Spirit of Now, peterrussell.com/pete.php

[62] Russell, Peter. "Is Reality All in the Mind?" Peter Russell- Spirit of Now, peterrussell.com/SCG/ideal.php

[63] Ibid.

[64] Rumi, Mewlana Jalaluddin. "The Guest House." Scottish Poetry Library, scottishpoetrylibrary.org.uk/poem/guest-house/

[65] Ibid.

[66] *Holy Bible*, New Living Translation. Carol Stream: Tyndale House Publishers, Inc., 1996 by Tyndale House Foundation. biblegateway.com/passage/?search=1+Corinthians+13&version=NLT

[67] *Little Buddha*. Directed by Bernardo Bertolucci. France/United Kingdom: Record Picture Company, 1993, amazon.com/dp/B00AM3EGPK

Chapter 7

[68] Doidge, Norman. The Brain That Changes Itself: Stories of Personal Triumph from the Frontiers of Brain Science. New York: Penguin Group, 2007, amazon.com/dp/0143113100

[69] "The Levels of Mind Teaching and Illustration" is used with permission from David Hoffmeister and the Foundation for the Awakening Mind. For more healing tools, please visit David's website, davidhoffmeister.com, which contains a variety of healing tools that he has shared over the years.

[70] "The Twelve Principles of Attitudinal Healing." Attitudinal Healing International, ahinternational.org/about/about-ahinternational/principles-of-attitudinal-healing

Chapter 8

[71] Senelick, Richard C. "Why Dying Is Different for Doctors." Life, HuffPost News. Published May 11, 2012. Updated July 11, 2012, huffpost.com/entry/doctors-death_n_1500871

[72] Guru is a common term in Hindi used to refer to a spiritual teacher, sage or master and *ji* is a suffix added to denote respect and regard.

[73] Campbell, Joseph and Moyers, Bill. *The Power of Myth*. New York City: Anchor Books, 1988, amazon.com /dp/0385418868

Chapter 9

[74] Food that is prepared to be blessed first by the gods or a Guru and then to be shared with others. Morales, Frank Gaetano. "*Prasada: Divine Food Offering*." Learn Religions. Updated April 29, 2019, thoughtco.com/prasada-divine-food-offering-1770685

[75] A garment consisting of a length of cotton or silk elaborately draped around the body, traditionally worn by women from South Asia.

Chapter 10

[76] An abnormal passageway had developed between the aorta (the biggest artery in the body) and the inferior vena cava (a large vein in the body).

[77] A Hindu term used to refer to God, or a guru or teacher who is revered, adored and highly esteemed and respected. "Bhagwan Definition- What does *Bhagwan* mean?" Yogapedia, yogapedia.com/definition/5400/bhagwan

[78] A traditional dress worn by various peoples of south-central Asia. Not only is it popular among women in India but is also worn by both men and women in Pakistan and Afghanistan (where they say *shalwar* instead

of *salwar*).

79 Shepard, Aaron. "The Princess and the God: A Tale of Ancient India." Aaron Shepard's World of Stories: Folktales, Fairy Tales, Tall Tales, Myths, Legends and More, aaronshep.com/stories/006.html

Chapter 11

80 Name changed to protect identity of child and her family.

81 Wiener, Jerry M. "Attitudes of pediatricians toward the care of fatally ill children." *The Journal of Pediatrics* Volume 76, number 5 (1970). 700-705, sciencedirect.com/science/article/pii/S0022347670802876

82 Khaneja, Seema and Milrod, Barbara. "Educational Needs Among Pediatricians Regarding Caring for Terminally Ill Children." *Archives of Pediatrics and Adolescent Medicine* Volume 152, number 9 (1998): 909-914, jamanetwork.com/journals/jamapediatrics/fullarticle/189837

83 *Mama* is a Hindi term used to address a maternal uncle, and *ji* is a suffix added to denote respect for an elder.

84 A long shirt and pants usually made of cotton that are everyday wear for men in India.

85 A traditional dress worn by various peoples of South and Central Asia. Not only is it popular among women in India but is also worn by both men and women in Pakistan and Afghanistan (where they say *shalwar* instead of *salwar*).

86 Swami Prabhavananda, Isherwood, Christopher, and Huxley, Aldous. *Bhagavad Gita: The Song of God.* New York: Signet Classic, 2002, amazon.com/dp/0451528441

87 If the word God does not feel comfortable for you, please feel free to substitute love, or peace or light, or whichever word or phrase that conveys the place within us that is whole, pure, innocent, eternal, and timeless. I invite you to not let the words used prevent you from truly opening to receive the profound wisdom and healing comfort of this lesson.

Chapter 12

88 In the clarification of terms in *A Course in Miracles*, *right-mindedness* is referred to as being in one's right mind where we listen to the voice for peace and love. (C-1.5:2)

Chapter 13

89 From the perspective of ACIM, the term *mind* includes the intellectual thinking mind, but also includes the emotions, feelings, beliefs and desires that form our perception of the world. The mind can be aware or

unaware, awake or sleeping. It can listen to only two voices: (1) love, which is our innate spiritual wisdom that is available to everyone, or (2) fear, which is the message of the ego that sees us as individual bodies separated not only from our innate inner wisdom but also disconnected from each other. ACIM refers to this as the right or wrong mind. As shared earlier, many students I work with feel that the terms *right* and *wrong* invoke a sense of self-judgment or judgment of other. For this reason, I have used the terms aware vs. unaware or awake vs. sleeping. The meaning however is the same as what is shared by ACIM.

[90] Miracle-mindedness is essentially being connected to the voice of our innate spiritual wisdom and seeing the world with this vision. The mind that is unaware of this innate spiritual wisdom lives in fear and needs help or healing so that it can be realigned. The miracle is a shift in perception from fear to love, thus serving the purpose of restoring the receiver to their aware mind.

[91] merriam-webster.com/dictionary/miracle

[92] oxforddictionaries.com/definition/miracle

Chapter 14

[93] Hay, Louise. *You Can Heal Your Life*. Carlsbad: Hay House, 1984, amazon.com/dp/0937611018

[94] If the term Holy Spirit does not feel comfortable to you, feel free to use another term such as inner guide, intuition, higher power, inner wisdom, the voice for love or peace, the still small voice, or whichever terms refer to that space deep inside each of us that guides us with love, wisdom, and compassion.

Chapter 15

[95] "So what are Obstacles to Cure?" The Center for Homeopathy of Southern Vermont, centerforhomeopathy.com/blog/so-what-are-obstacles-to-cure

[96] Hoffmeister, David. "A Course in Miracles is to be Lived, David Hoffmeister, ACIM." YouTube video, 14:55. Posted [May 2013], youtu.be/M3DFwnK4f2w

[97] Sentis. "Neuroplasticity." YouTube video, 2:03. Posted [November 2012], youtu.be/ELpfYCZa87g

[98] Fossella, Tina. Human Nature, Buddha Nature: On Spiritual Bypassing, Relationship, and the Dharma - An interview with John Welwood. John Welwood. Integrating Western Psychology with Eastern Spiritual Wisdom.

[99] "At the Heart of Healing: Connection." Ornish Lifestyle Medicine, ornish.com/proven-program/love-support/

Chapter 16

[100] "Levels of Mind Process — Your Instrument to Peace." Levels of Mind: The Fast Track to Enlightenment, levelsofmind.com/levels-of-mind-process/

[101] Khaneja, Seema. "Finding your own inner GPS: Reclaiming the inner power of YOU." Coaching for Inner Peace. Published April 13, 2016, coachingforinnerpeace.com/coaching-for-inner-peace/finding-inner-gps-reclaiming-inner-power/

[102] Khaneja, Seema and Hoffmeister, David. "Levels of Mind: Your Very Own GPS — An Interview with David Hoffmeister." Coaching for Inner Peace. Published May 14, 2016, coachingforinnerpeace.com/course-in-miracles/levels-mind-gps-interview-david-hoffmeister/

[103] "The Levels of Mind Teaching and Illustration" is used with permission from David Hoffmeister and the Foundation for the Awakening Mind. For more healing tools, please visit David's website, davidhoffmeister.com, which contains a variety of healing tools that he has shared over the years.

Chapter 17

[104] Name changed for client confidentiality.

[105] Chodron, Pema. When Things Fall Apart: Heart Advice for Difficult Times. Boston: Shambhala Library, 2002, amazon.com/dp/1570629692

Chapter 18

[106] dictionary.cambridge.org/dictionary/english/commitment

[107] When I refer to mind, I include our perceptions, emotions, thoughts, beliefs and our desires.

[108] Shapiro, Fred. R. "Who Wrote the Serenity Prayer?" The Chronicle of Higher Education. Published April 2014. chronicle.com/article/Who-Wrote-the-Serenity-Prayer-/146159/

About the Author

Seema Khaneja graduated from the Mt. Sinai School of Medicine in New York City and completed her residency in pediatrics at New York Hospital-Cornell Medical Center. During medical school and after residency, she studied various complementary healing modalities including Ayurvedic nutrition, mind-body medicine, yoga and meditation. For ten years, Seema practiced holistic medicine, caring for children and adults, with a focus on chronic physical and mental health challenges. She facilitated numerous classes in meditation, stress management, and holistic medicine for medical students at the University of Rochester Medical School as well as the local lay community in Rochester, New York, where she resides. She is also a Clinical Instructor at the University of Rochester's Department of Pediatrics.

Born in India, she spent her early childhood years there. Since her teenage years, Seema studied with spiritual teachers in the Hindu and Buddhist tradition, and is also a student of *A Course in Miracles*. She completed a two-year online Mystical Mind Training through Living Church Ministries and became a Commissioned Minister in the spring of 2019.

Seema created Coaching for Inner Peace to help clients move through emotional and physical health challenges using their inner spiritual resources in a way that is deeply transformative and immensely practical. She also is the Director of Shanti Academy, an online learning portal offering courses for students seeking a pragmatic and concrete way to experience inner peace.

Seema is passionate about integrating the wisdom of world spiritual traditions with scientific research, to guide people to holistic healing. In her leisure time, she loves to take walks by the Erie Canal, create new Indian-Western vegetarian fusion recipes in her kitchen, and watch movies (Bollywood and Hollywood) with her friends and family.

Thank you for reading my book, *Physician, Heal Thyself.*

I hope you found inspiration and value in it. If so, please tell your friends—word of mouth is an author's best friend. You can share an honest review on your blog, leave links on your social media sites, or review it on Amazon. Thanks, again!

For more information about me and
Coaching for Inner Peace, enjoy my website,
CoachingForInnerPeace.com